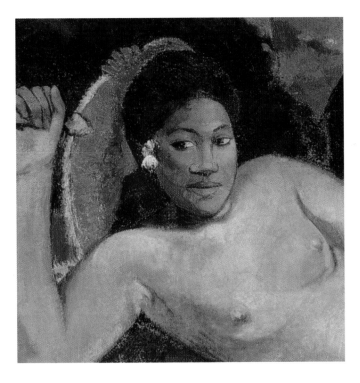

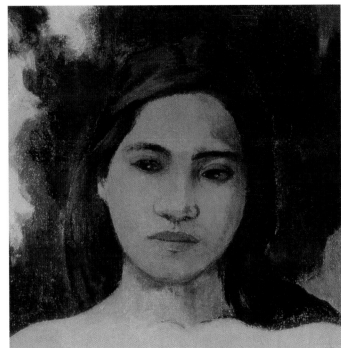

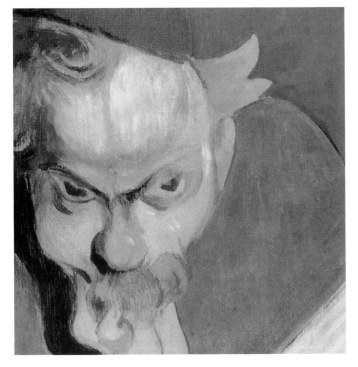

Cover: Stéphanie Angoh
Page layout: Julien Depaulis

© Confidential Concepts, worldwide, USA, 2003
© Sirocco, London, 2003 (English version)

Published in 2003 by Grange Books
an imprint of Grange Books Plc
The Grange Kingsnorth Industrial Estate
Hoo, nr Rochester Kent ME3 9ND
www.Grangebooks.co.uk
ISBN 1-84013-560-3

Paul

Gauguin

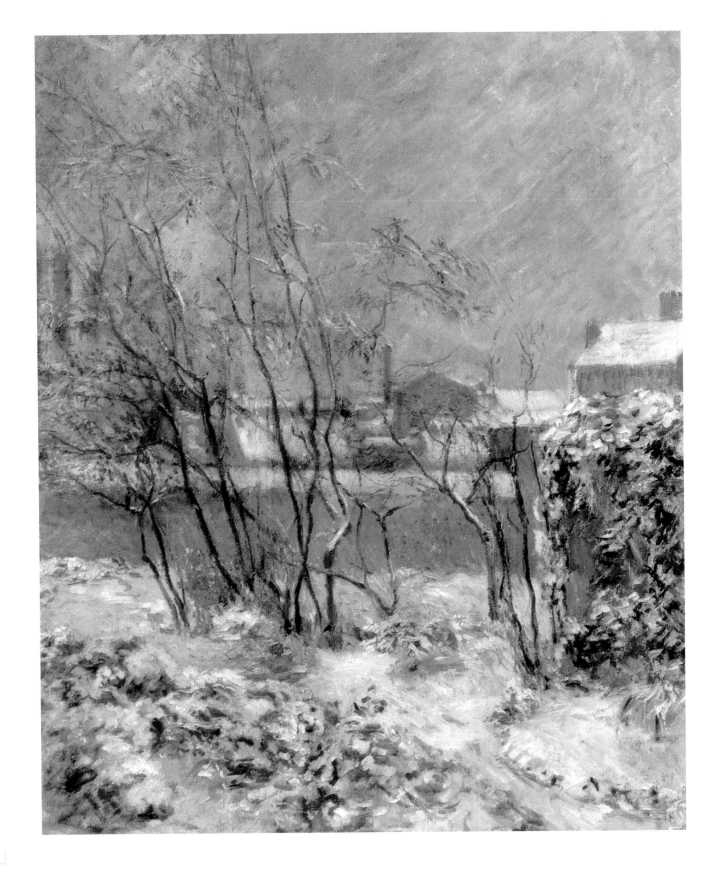

On 8 May 1903, having lost a futile and fatally exhausting battle with colonial officials, threatened with a ruinous fine and an imprisonment for allegedly instigating the natives to mutiny and slandering the authorities, after a week of acute physical sufferings endured in utter isolation, an artist who had devoted himself to glorifying the pristine harmony of Oceania's tropical nature and its people died. There is bitter irony in the name given by Gauguin to his house at Atuona – "Maison du Jouir" (House of Pleasure) – and in the words carved on its wood reliefs, *Soyez amoureuses et vous serez heureuses* (Be in love and you will be happy) and *Soyez mystérieuses* (Be mysterious).

In his regular report to Paris, the bishop wrote: "The only noteworthy event here has been the sudden death of a contemptible individual named Gauguin, a reputed artist but an enemy of God and everything that is decent.[1]" It was only twenty years later that the artist's name appeared on his tombstone, and even that belated honour was due to a curious circumstance: Gauguin's grave was found by a painter belonging to the Society of American Fakirs.

It was only due to the presence of a few travellers and colonists who knew something about art and to the ill-concealed greediness of his recent enemies who, for all their hate, did not shrink from making money on his works, that part of Gauguin's artistic legacy escaped destruction. For example, the gendarme of Atuona who had personally supervised the sale and destroyed with his own hands some of the artist's works which supposedly offended his chaste morals, was not above purloining a few pictures and later upon his return to Europe, opened a kind of Gauguin museum. As the result of all this, not one of Gauguin's works remains in Tahiti.

The news of Gauguin's death, which reached France with a four-month delay, evoked an unprecedented interest in his life and work. The artist's words about posthumous fame came true. He shared the fate of many artists who received recognition when they could no longer enjoy it. Daniel de Monfreid predicted this in a letter written to Gauguin several months before his death: "In returning you will risk damaging that process of incubation which is taking place in the public's appreciation of you.

1. **Snow Effects** (*Snow in Rue Carcel*), 1882-1883. Oil on canvas, 60 x 50 cm. Ny Carlsberg Glyptotek, Copenhagen.

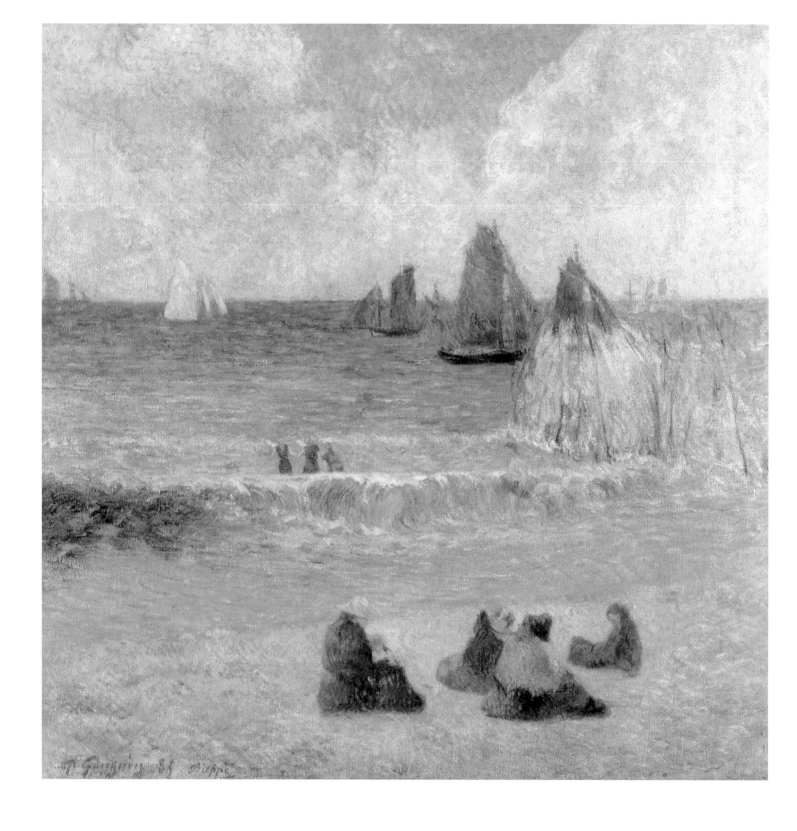

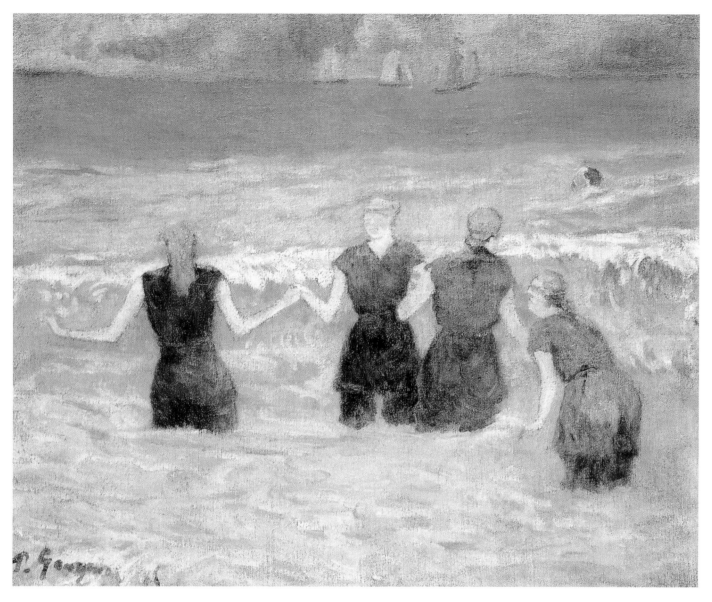

You are now that unprecedented legendary artist, who from the furthest South Seas sends his disturbing, inimitable works, the definitive works of a great man who has, as it were, disappeared from the world. Your enemies – and like all who upset the mediocrity you have many enemies – are silent: they dare not attack you, do not even think of it. You are so far away. You should not return. You should not deprive them of the bone they hold in their teeth. You are already unassailable like all the great dead; you already belong to the history of art.[2] "

2. *Dieppe Beach*, *1885*. Oil on canvas, 38 x 46 cm. National Museum of Western Art, Tokyo.

3. *Bathers in Dieppe*, 1885. Oil on canvas, 71.5 x 71.5 cm. Ny Carlsberg Glyptotek, Copenhagen.

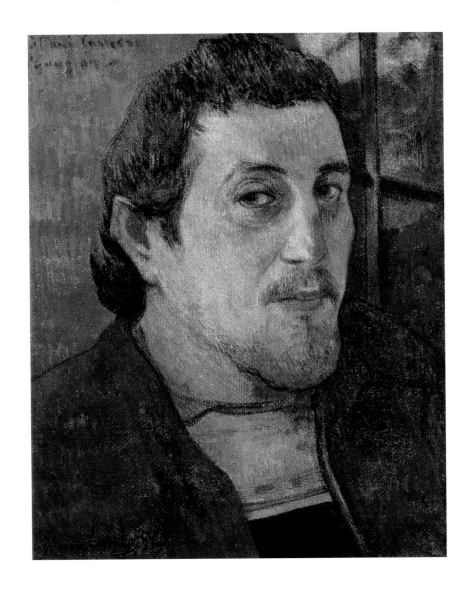

In the same year 1903, Ambroise Vollard exhibited at his Paris gallery about a hundred paintings and drawings by Gauguin. Some had been sent to him by the artist from Oceania, others had been purchased from various art dealers and collectors. In 1906, in Paris, a Gauguin retrospective was held at the newly opened Salon d'Automne. Two hundred and twenty-seven works (not counting those listed in the catalogue without numbers) were put on display – painting, graphic art, pottery, and woodcarving. Octave Maus, the leading Belgian art critic, wrote on this occasion: "Paul Gauguin is a great colourist, a great draughtsman, a great decorator; a versatile and self-confident painter.[3]" When it comes to the question of accepting or rejecting his artistic credo or of determining his place in art, the

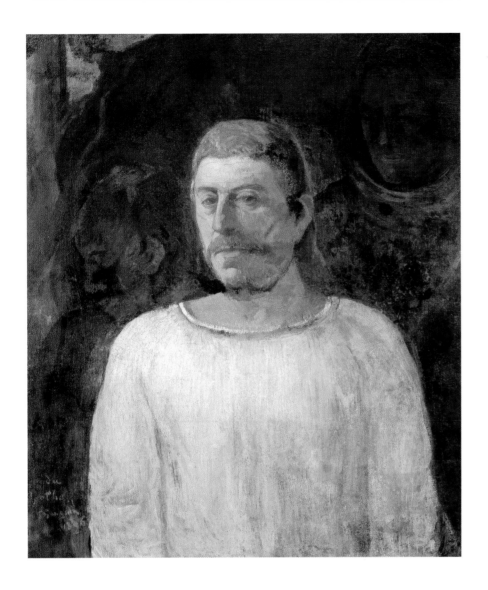

different, even mutually exclusive views expressed by different generations of researchers with different aesthetic tastes are quite justified. Some experts see Gauguin as a destroyer of realism who denounced traditions and paved the way for "free art", be it Fauvism, Expressionism, Surrealism or Abstractionism. Others, on the contrary, think that Gauguin continued the European artistic tradition. Some contemporaries reacted to his departure from Europe with mistrust and suspicion, for they believed that a true artist could and must work only on his native soil and not derive inspiration from an alien culture. Pissarro, Cézanne and Renoir shared this opinion, for example. They considered Gauguin's borrowings from the stylistics of Polynesian culture to be a kind of plunder.

5. *Self-Portrait at Golgotha*, 1886. Oil on canvas, 74 x 64 cm. Museu de Arte, Saõ Paulo.

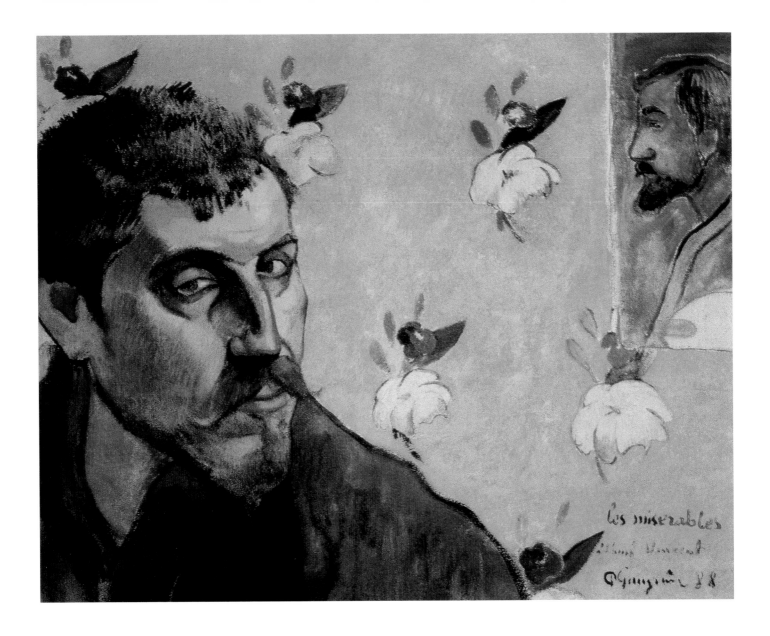

6. *Self-Portrait, "Les Misérables"*, 1888. Oil on canvas, 45 x 55 cm. Rijksmuseum Vincent van Gogh, Amsterdam.

Such controversial opinions of Gauguin's art are by no means accidental. His life and work present many contradictions, though often only outward ones. His life was naturally integrated with his creative activity, while the latter in its turn embodied his ideals and views on life. But this organic unity of life and work was maintained through a never-ending dramatic struggle. It was the struggle for the right to become an artist, the struggle for existence, the struggle against public opinion, against his family and friends who failed to understand him, and finally, it was his inner struggle for the

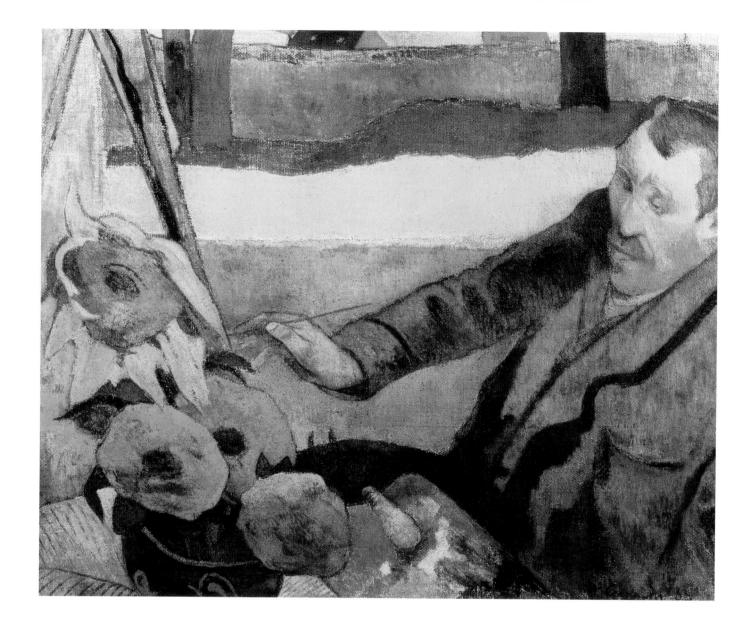

preservation of his identity, his own creative and human self. Gauguin could hardly have become an artist who "reinvented painting" (Maurice Malingue) and who "initiated the art of modern times" (René Huyghe).

Gauguin began his career as a grown man. Nothing in his childhood or youth betrayed any hint of his future as an artist. He was born in Paris on 7 June 1848, in the midst of the revolutionary events when barricade fighting was going on in the streets of the city. This fact was to have repercussions for Gauguin's later life.

7. *Van Gogh Painting Sunflowers*, 1888.
Oil on canvas,
73 x 92 cm.
Rijksmuseum Vincent van Gogh, Amsterdam.

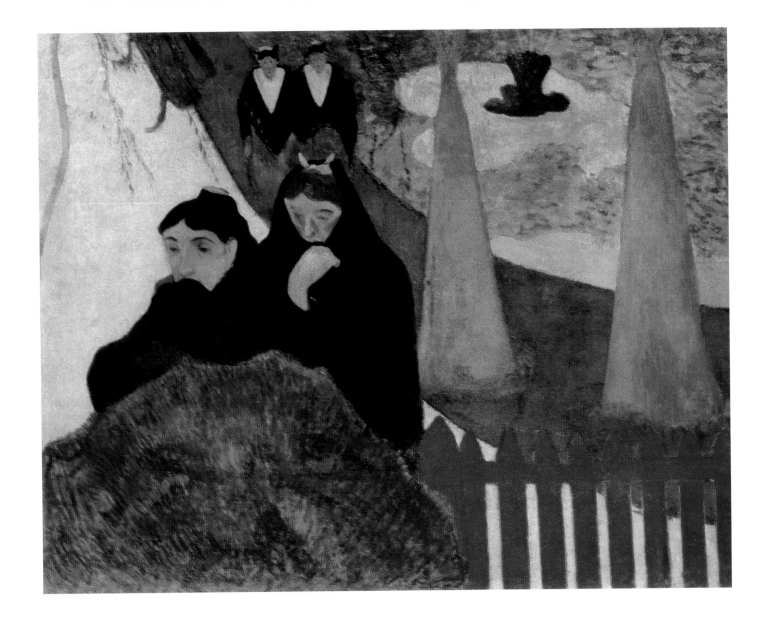

8. **Old Women in Arles**
(in the Arles Hospital Garden), 1888.
Oil on canvas,
73 x 92 cm. Art
Institute, Chicago.

It is difficult to say whether Clovis Gauguin played an active role in the events, but it is a fact that following the failure of Marrast (who was a member of General Cavaignac's government) in the election to the National Assembly, the Gauguins left France. In the autumn of 1849, the family sailed for Peru, where they could count on the support of Mine Gauguin's distant but influential relatives. On 30 October 1849, he died at sea and his wife, with two children, had to continue the journey on her own. Childhood in Peru was forever engraved on Paul Gauguin's memory. The recollections of simple, natural

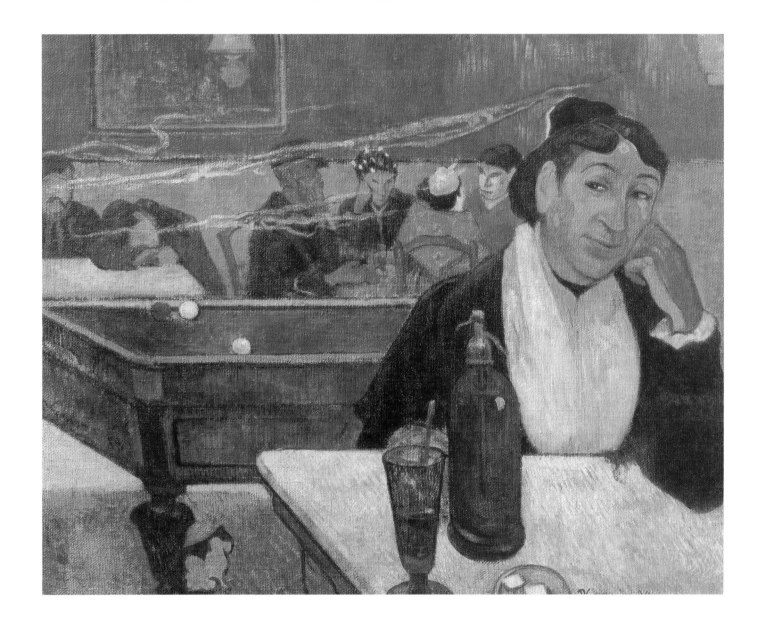

relations among people with different-coloured skins, who lacked racial or social prejudice, the relations, which might have been largely idealized in the child's memory, merged with the recollections of luxuriant tropical nature with its rich colours under the dazzling sun. It is very likely that these early impressions determined the subsequent development of Gauguin's artistic tastes and ideals. Return to France put an end to Paul's happy and carefree life. At school in Orleans and later at a Lycée in Paris the dream of tropical countries and the sea never left Gauguin.

9. *Café at Arles*, 1888. Oil on canvas, 72 x 92 cm. Pushkin Museum of Fine Arts, Moscow.

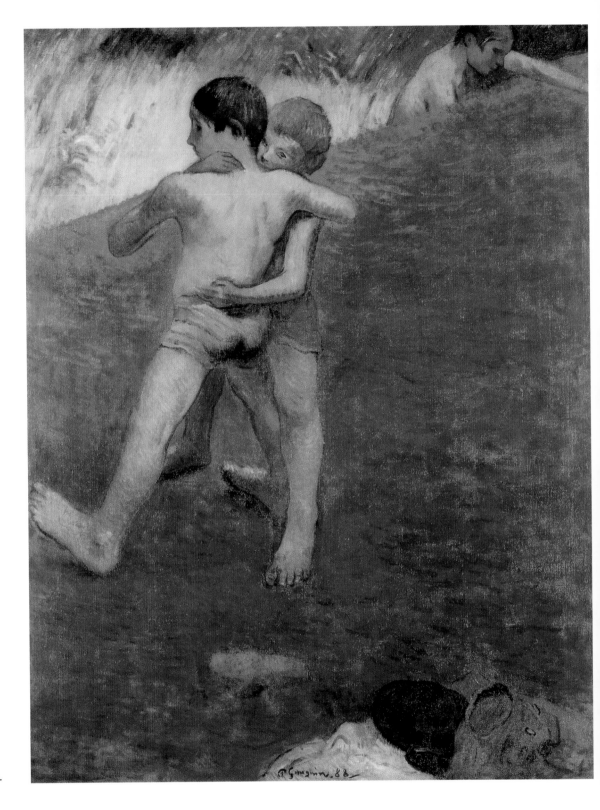

10. *Fighting Children*,
1888. Oil on canvas,
93 x 73 cm. Private
Collection, Lausanne.

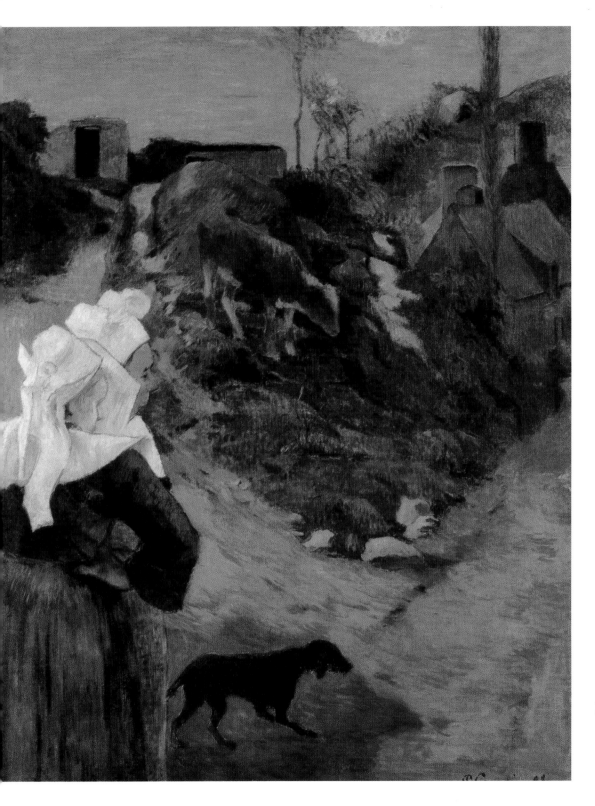

11. *Bretons and Calf*,
    1888. Oil on canvas,
    91 x 72 cm.
    Ny Glyptotek,
    Copenhagen.

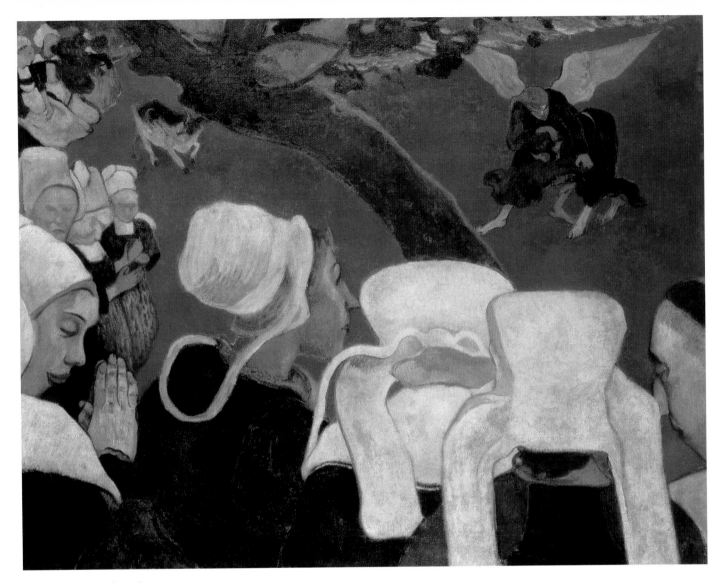

12. *The Vision after the Sermon or Jacob Fighting with the Angel*, 1888. Oil on canvas, 73 x 92 cm. Private Collection, Lausanne.

13. *Blue Trees*, 1888. Oil on canvas, 92 x 73 cm. Ordrurgaards-Amlingen, Copenhagen.

At fifteen he found employment as a cabin-boy on a merchant ship and sailed to the South American coast, almost retracing the route of his first voyage overseas. But this romantic start was followed by an abrupt and unwelcome change: the Franco-Prussian war broke out, the merchant ship on which Gauguin served was requisitioned, and instead of the tropics he found himself in the north, near the Norwegian and Danish coasts. In April 1871, after the disbandment of the French forces, Gauguin returned to Paris with a third-class seaman's diploma. His mother was dead, the house at St. Cloud plundered and gutted by fire. In search of work Gauguin turned to his sister's guardian Gustave Arosa who helped him to become a stockbroker at the Bertin bank.

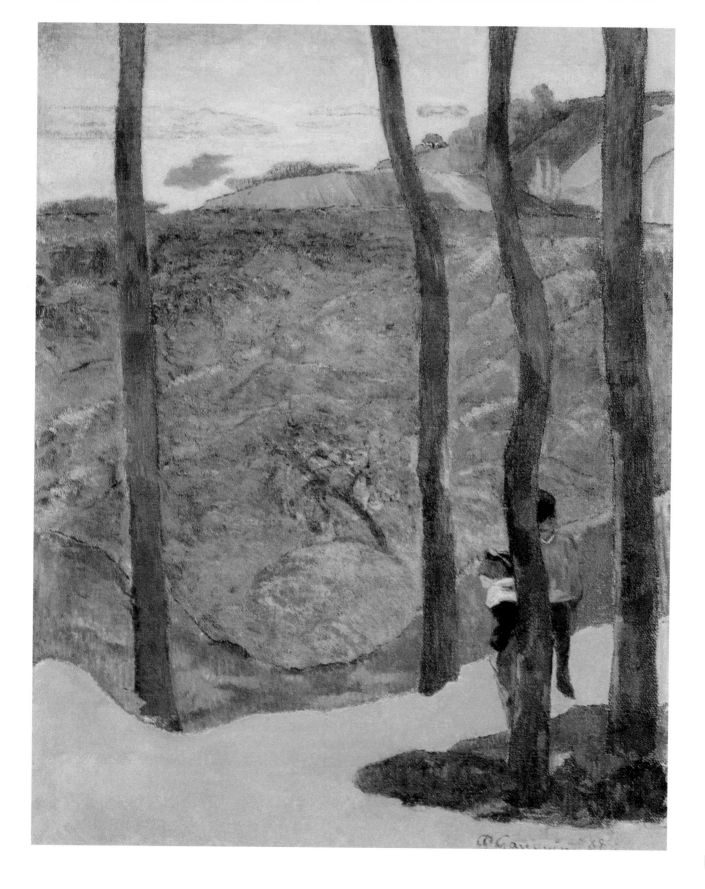

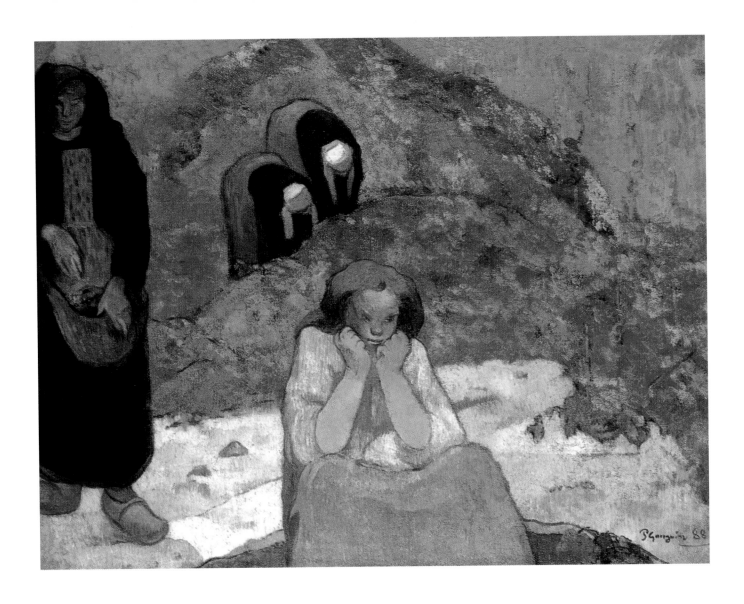

14. ***Human Miseries***
    (Vineyards), 1888.
    Oil on canvas,
    73 x 92 cm.
    Ordurupgaardsamlingen,
    Copenhagen.

He quickly made a success as a businessman, settled down to raise a family, bought a house and began to lead the orderly life of typical bourgeois. The only thing that set him apart from others of his circle was his unorthodox interest in art. It might have been stimulated by the atmosphere in Arosa's house as the owner loved painting and photography and kept a splendid collection of pictures.

A friend of Arosa's, Nadar was a cartoonist and photographer and it was in his studio that the first exhibition of the Impressionists took place. The earliest known landscape by Gauguin is dated 1871. It was done in oils and was probably a product of the painting lessons which Gauguin attended together with Arosa's daughter Marguerite.

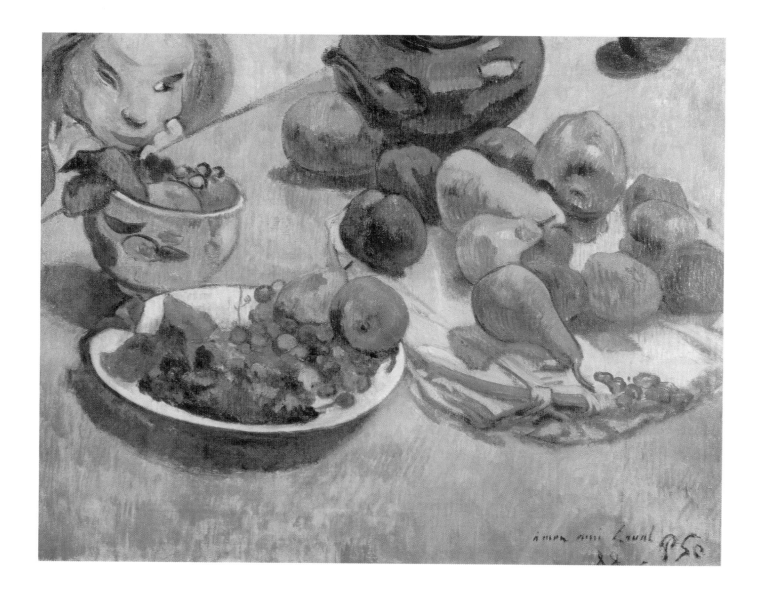

Arosa's example as well as his own inclination encouraged Gauguin to form a collection of pictures. Although small in size, it fairly accurately reflected his artistic taste: Manet and Monet, Pissarro and Cézanne, Renoir and Sisley – painters who had very few admirers at that time. A decisive part in Gauguin's initiation into art, and especially into Impressionist painting, was played by Pissarro, who willingly advised him on both the theory and technique of painting, and actually instructed him when they worked side by side painting the same motif. At Pissarro's studio Gauguin also met Cézanne who strongly appealed to him both as a person and as an artist, and whose work greatly influenced his own.

15. *Fruit*, 1888.
Oil on canvas,
43 x 58 cm. The
Pushkin Museum of
Fine Arts, Moscow.

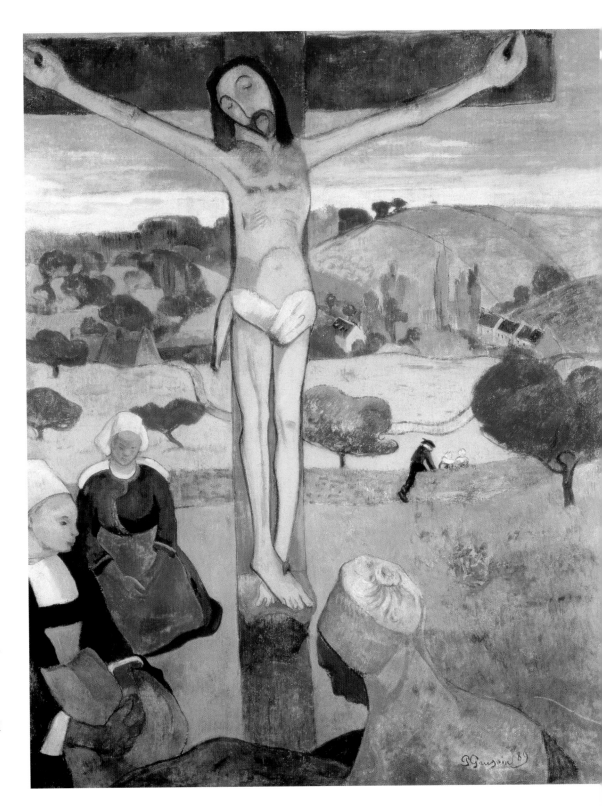

16. *The Yellow Christ*,
    1889. Oil on canvas,
    113 x 92 cm, Narodni
    Gallery, Prague.

17. *Hello, Mr Gauguin*,
    1889. Oil on canvas,
    113 x 92 cm. Narodni
    Gallery, Prague.

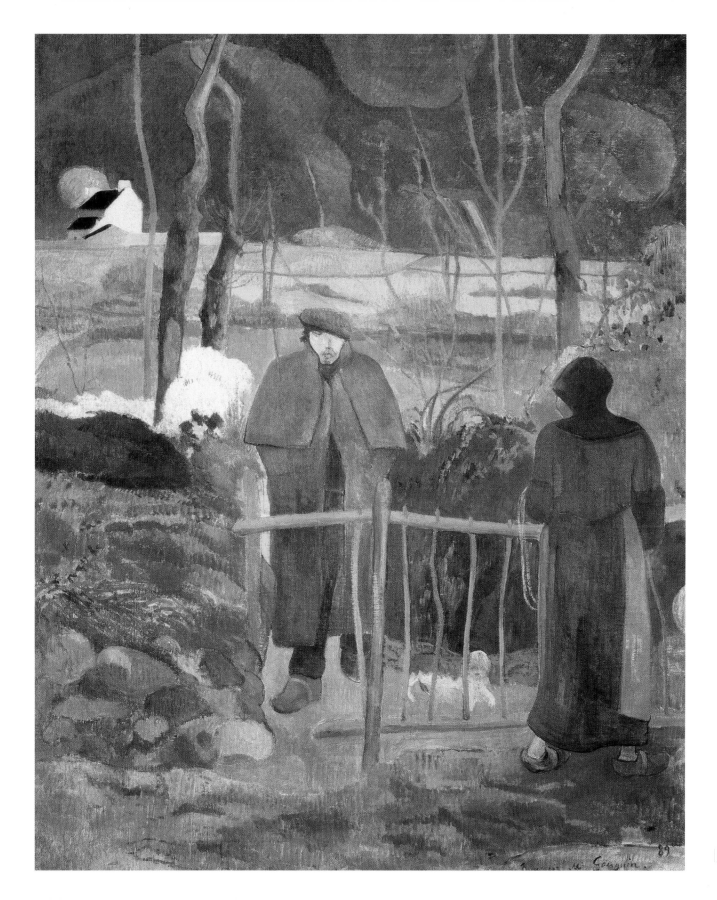

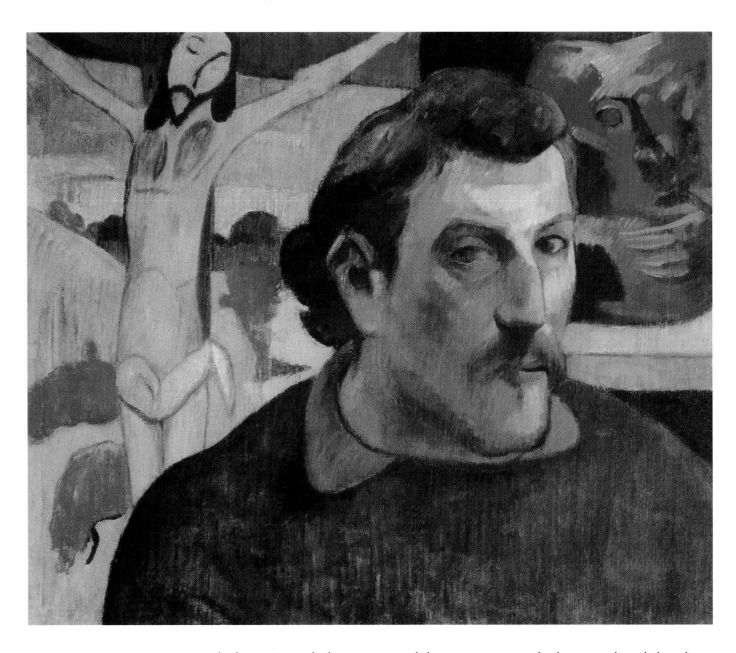

18. *Self-Portrait with the Yellow Christ*, 1889. Oil on canvas, 92 x 73 cm. Albright-Knox Gallery, Buffalo.

No doubt, it was with this aim in mind that Gauguin rented a house and workshop first from the ceramist and jeweller Jean-Paul Aubé, and then from the sculptor Jules Ernest Bouillot. While working at the latter's studio, Gauguin produced, first in plaster and then in marble, bust portraits of his wife and son. In 1876, Gauguin exhibited a landscape at the Salon and received a favourable press. From 1879 onwards, he contributed to the Impressionist shows and actively engaged in organizational work, inviting new artists to exhibit with the group.

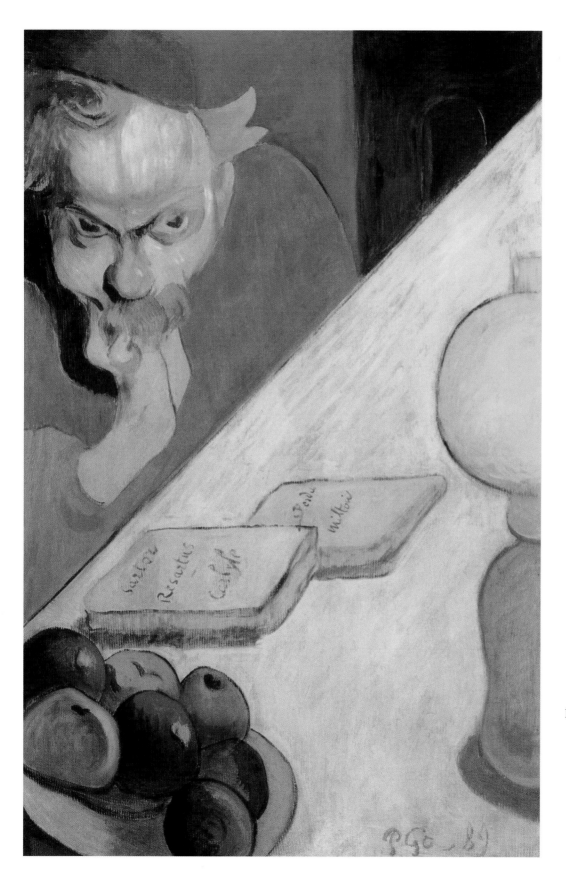

19. ***Portrait of Meyer de Haan***, 1889.
Oil on canvas,
80 x 52 cm. Private
Collection.

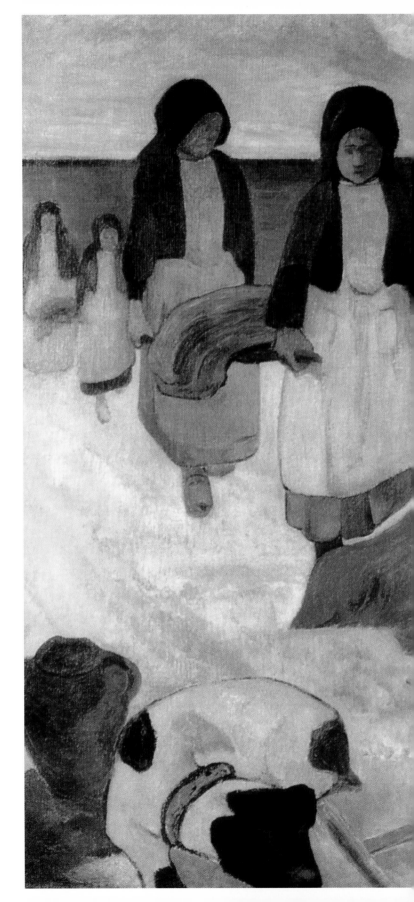

20. *Wrach Collectors*,
 1889. Oil on canvas,
 87 x 122.5 cm.
 Folkwang Museum,
 Essen.

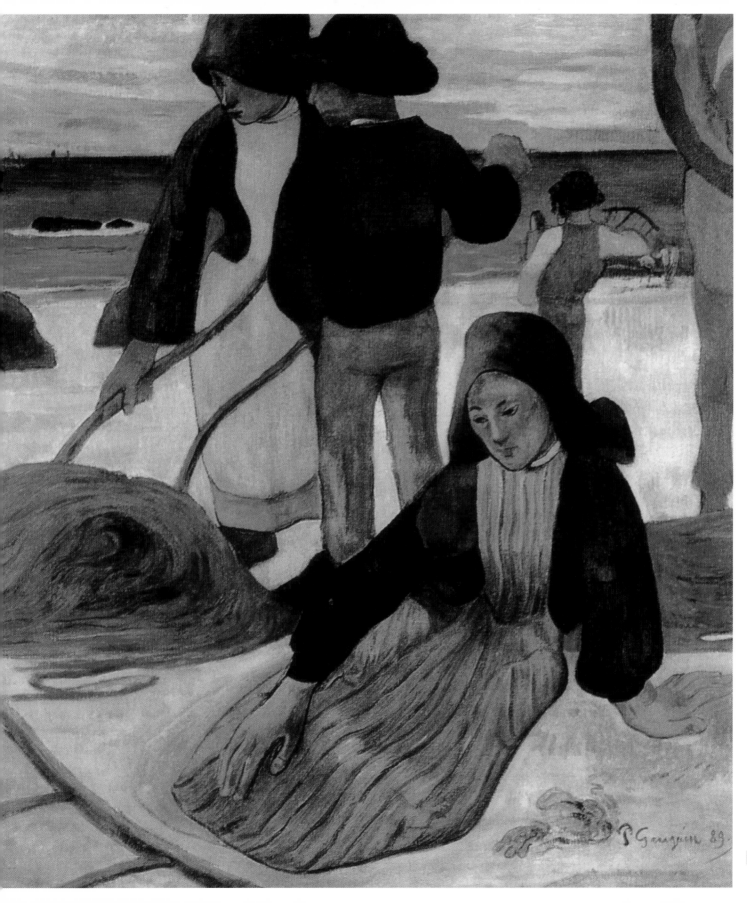

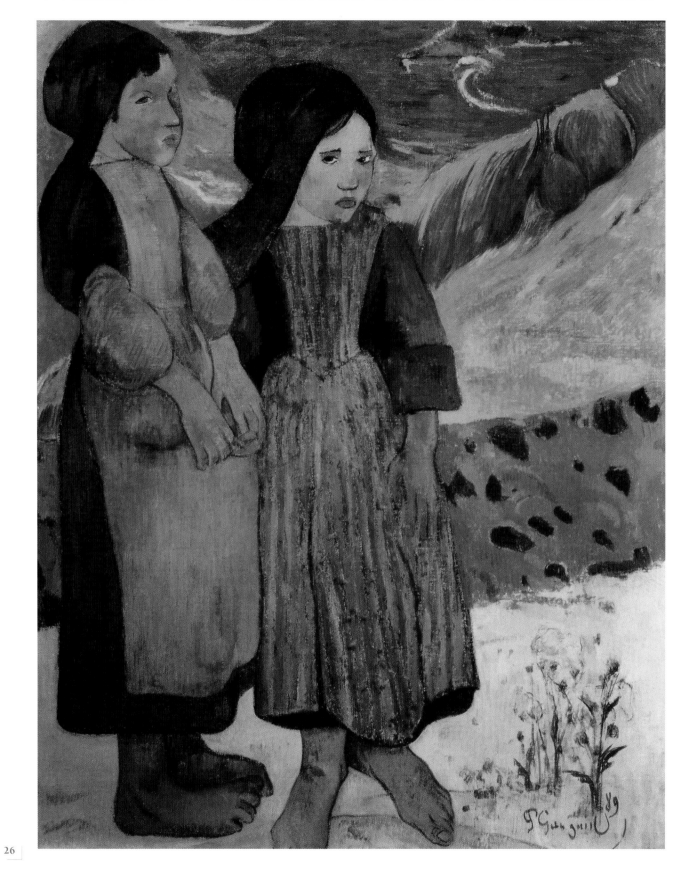

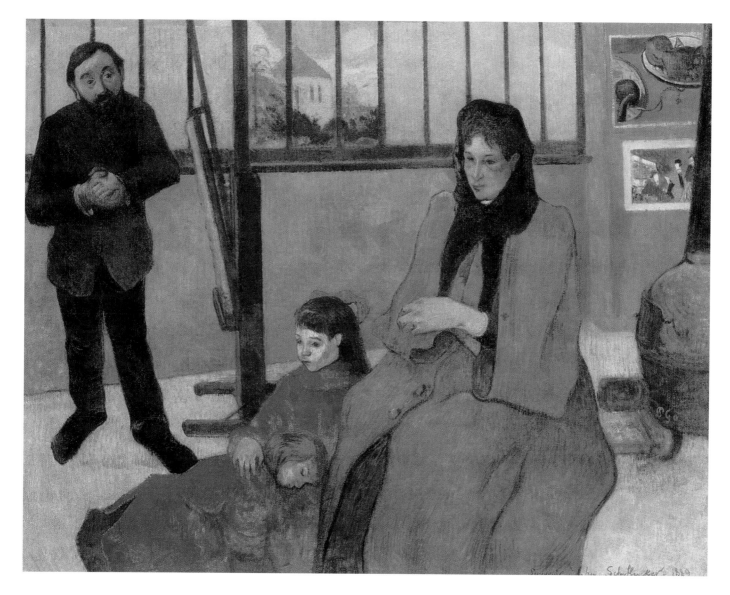

Art was gradually ousting all other interests in Gauguin's life, and when, in 1883, he was obliged to resign his job at Bertin's due to a financial crisis, it was not without joy – albeit not without apprehension either – that he decided to give up his banking career for good. He decided to go to Copenhagen, his wife's native city. His Danish inlaws felt duty bound to make him see reason and accept a place in a company selling horse-cloths and canvas. Gauguin's attitude provoked open hostility, and as a result, in the summer of 1885, leaving his wife Mette Gad and four of their children behind, Gauguin returned to Paris with his six-year-old son. From now on his only purpose in life was to become an artist, and not just any artist, but an outstanding one.

21. ***Breton Children on the Seaside***, 1889. Oil on canvas, 92 x 73 cm. National Museum of Western Art, Tokyo.

22. ***The Schuffenecker Family***, 1889. Oil on canvas, 73 x 92 cm. Musée d'Orsay, Paris.

The earliest period in Gauguin's artistic career which began with his Sunday lessons in professional skills, was closely linked with Impressionism. For Gauguin, the "Impressionist is pure, not yet sullied by the putrid kiss of the Ecole des Beaux-Arts.[4]" This attitude prompted him to call the 1889 exhibition at the Cafe Volpini "Peinture du Groupe Impressionniste et Synthétiste", thus emphasizing the challenge to conventional salon painting. And the fact that Gauguin had found his way into art through Impressionism was of paramount importance for his further development, even though he later broke away from his teachers more decisively and uncompromisingly than any other of the Post-Impressionists. The main lesson he learnt from Impressionism was the rejection of the time-tested but antiquated traditions and the trust in the artist's own visual experience. Gauguin worked in the open air and applied his paints in small, brightly coloured dabs. He used the motifs and compositional devices of the Impressionists and discussed the issues which were important to them.

Gauguin felt the necessity to break out of the confines of Impressionism. The shimmering light which dissolved the outlines of figures and objects, and the flickering touch combined with the brightness of colour gave way to a dense brushwork and a reserved, rather dark palette, which at time brings an element of drama to the composition.

Gauguin's deviation from Impressionism first manifested itself during his stay in Rouen. It is particularly evident in his plastic works, a case in point being the carving of a small wooden jewellery box. This interest in the artist's inner feelings, in conveying an abstract idea instead of his visual impressions, was far removed from the Impressionist conception. Gauguin's stay in Copenhagen, far from his recent fellow artists, stimulated him to form an independent opinion of his art which, by his own admission, was rather "one of thought than of acquired technique.[5]"

According to Gauguin in a letter to his old friend Emile Schuffenecker (14 January 1885): "In my opinion, the great artist is the formulator of the greatest intelligence. The sentiments which occur to him are the most delicate and, consequently, the most invisible products, or translations, of the mind…"

Gauguin's infatuation with Delacroix was symptomatic in many respects. In contrast to some of his contemporaries, who, like Paul Signac – the founder of Neo-Impressionism – mostly admired Delacroix as a colourist, Gauguin saw his strength in his expressive and vigorous drawing which endowed his paintings with vitality and dramatic tension. However, no matter whether Gauguin owed any of his new artistic views to Delacroix or not, it should be noted that in his letters written in early 1885 he formulated, albeit not very consistently, the fundamental principles of an aesthetic system which was to be developed and implemented in his later work and which he himself termed "synthetism".

23. *Te avae no maria,*
    The Month of Mary
    (*or Woman Carrying Flowers*), 1889.
    Oil on canvas,
    97 x 72 cm.
    The Hermitage,
    St. Petersburg.

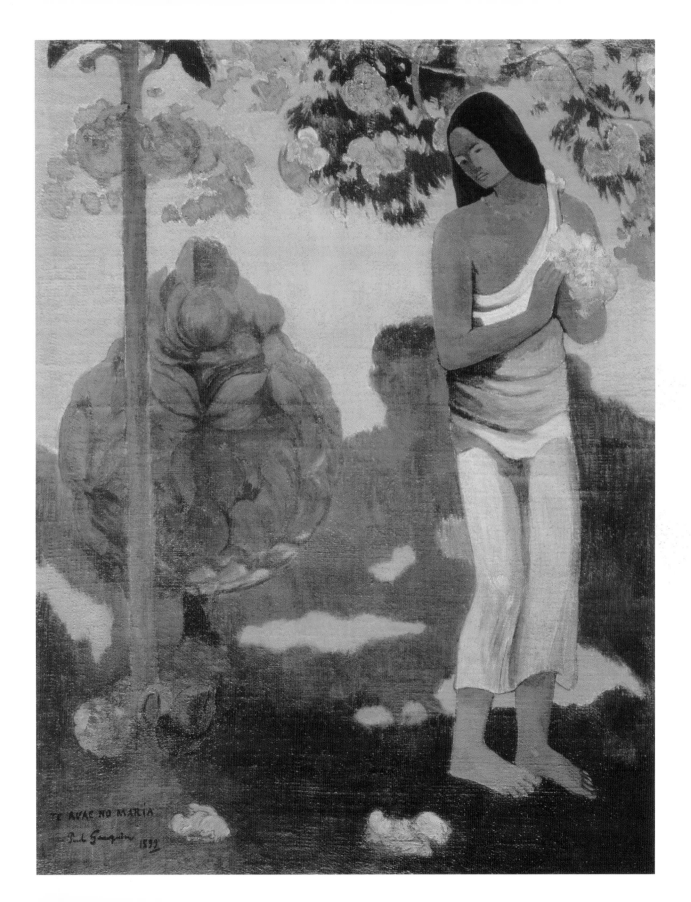

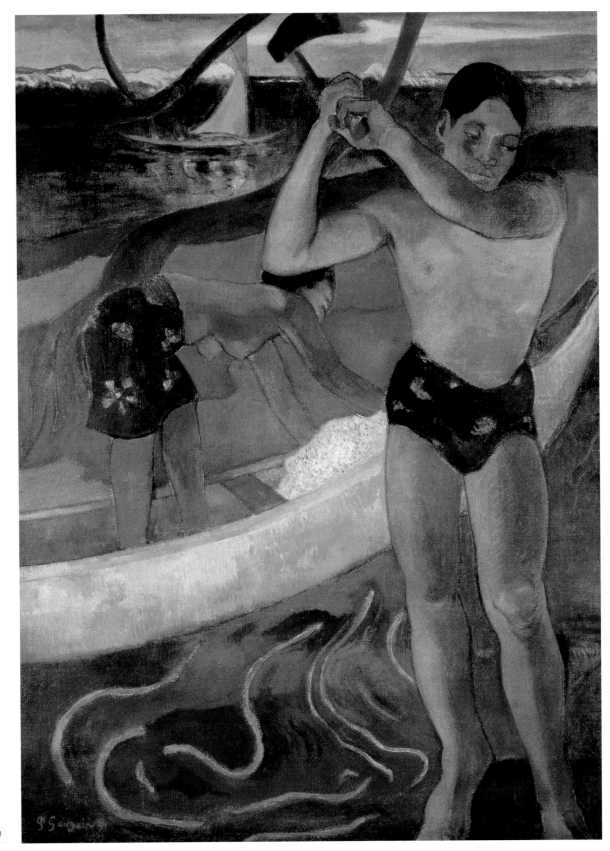

The year spent in Paris after his return from Copenhagen was one of the hardest in the artist's life. To support his son and pay the rent he had to earn money by pasting posters. However, he was able to contribute 19 paintings to the Impressionist exhibition in May 1886. He installed his son in a private boarding-school and he left for Brittany. The life at Pont-Aven gave the artist relative freedom and an opportunity to think over certain issues which had long preoccupied him. Gauguin spent about six months in Pont-Aven, a small, god-forsaken place lying at the foot of two large hills. Everything in that land – its archaic way of life, its heathen-flavoured Christian monuments and its dour hard-working peasants – mirrored Gauguin's own unhappy mood. Strictly speaking, this manner was not entirely new, for it had first manifested itself in works done in Dieppe where he had spent a few weeks in the summer of 1885 after leaving Denmark. Evidence of this can be found in three canvases: *The Harbour at Dieppe* (City Art Gallery, Manchester), *The Beach at Dieppe* (Ny Carlsberg Glyptotek, Copenhagen) and *Women Bathing* (National Museum of Western Art, Tokyo). The order of their painting is unknown, but stylistically they may be assigned to three different periods. While the Harbour is a purely Impressionist work, the Beach combines Impressionist features with a novel treatment of space. The third picture bears no trace of Impressionism. Gauguin's stay in Brittany saw a further development of his new style. The flickering light and air of his earlier pictures gave way to flat forms. Civilization and individual freedom, particularly the freedom of a creative personality, were for him incompatible notions. Unlike other painters, including the Impressionists, he never made the city the subject of his pictures. But his idea of leaving Paris had nothing to do with a rural idyll: he dreamt of distant tropical lands inhabited by free people, by savages unspoilt by the European civilization. These tropical fancies, born in the very first year of his financial troubles, were to stir his imagination from that time on with pictures of luxuriant and abundant nature, amongst which he saw himself living as a savage. His first contact with the reality, when in 1887, together with the young painter Charles Laval, he went to Panama, proved the ephemeral character of these dreams.

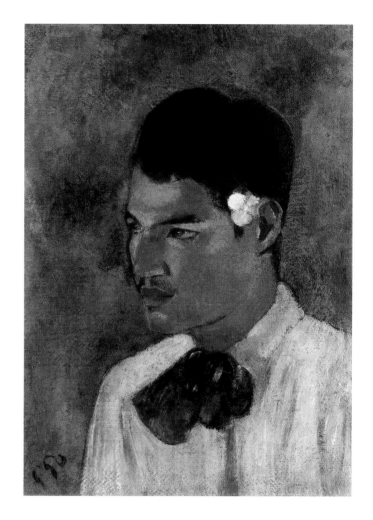

24. *Man with an Axe*, 1891. Oil on canvas, 92 x 70 cm. Private Collection.

25. *Young Tahitian Man* (*Young Man with a Flower*), 1891. Oil on canvas, 46 x 33 cm. Private Collection.

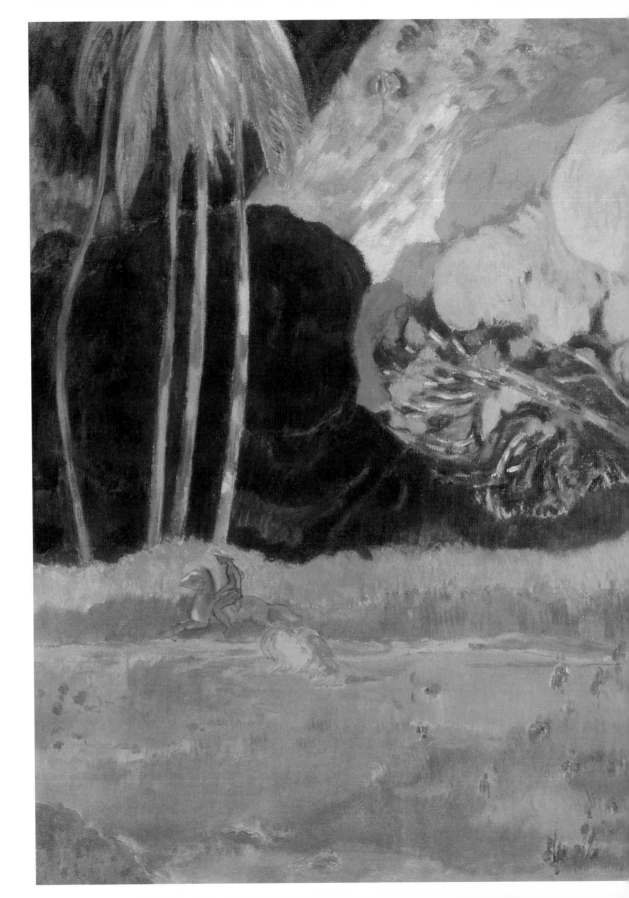

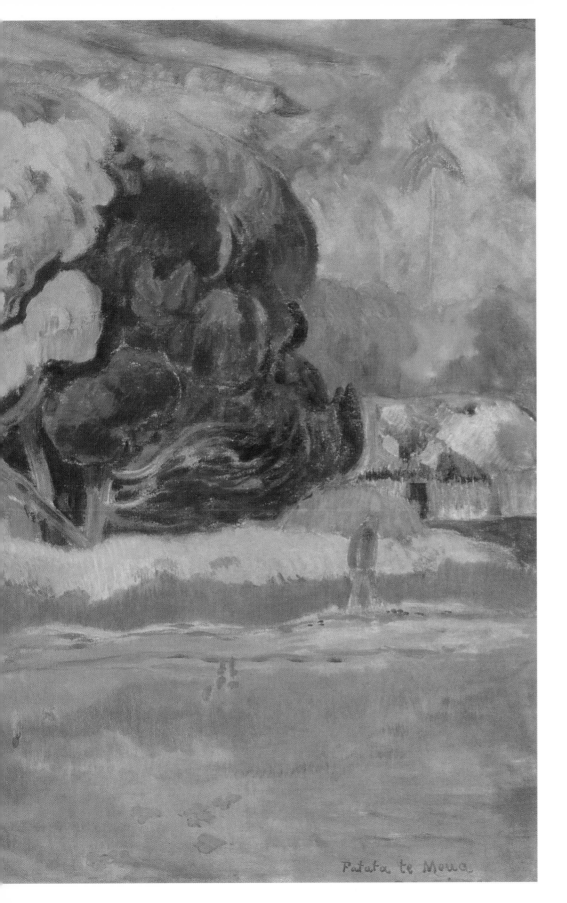

Fatata te Moua

26. ***Fatata te moua*** *(At the Foot of the Mountain or The Big Tree),* 1891. Oil on canvas, 67 x 91 cm. The Hermitage, St. Petersburg.

He had to change his brush for a spade to earn money for his passage – this time to Martinique which lured him with the same dream of a happy life, an opportunity to devote himself to painting, and of a family reunion. But in less than six months a fatal lack of money and tropical fever forced him to return to Paris.

However Gauguin's stay on Martinique turned out to be extremely important, for it finally freed him from Impressionism. Nature itself showed that it could be viewed from more than just the Impressionist angle: it offered a wealth and variety that called for a different pictorial system. The tropical sun revealed new possibilities in the rendering of light, space, volume and colour. Hence Gauguin's new tendency to concentrate large pools of contrasting colour to stress contours and smooth, expressive lines. "I have never before made paintings so clear, so lucid [6]", he wrote to Schuffenecker. After Martinique, he remained forever faithful to the arabesque – that 'thread of Ariadne', as it was dubbed by René Huyghe, which proved so important in his future work particularly in the development of cloisonnism or synthetism.

This new, real Gauguin failed to conceal his quest for a different, a non-European imagery – both in his art and in his life. To preserve moral strength for his work, he did not allow himself to get involved in any kind of emotional experience outside his creative pursuits and replied to his wife's complaints with the following words: "There are two natures in me: the Indian and the sensitive. The sensitive has disappeared, which permits the Indian to walk straight ahead firmly [7]".

Gauguin set to work in his own way. He rejected the potter's wheel and used the primitive method of hand-moulding. And indeed, Gauguin regarded ceramics not as a craft, but as an art in its own right, a sacred creative process whose secrets he was trying to disclose through experiments with shapes and colours. Yet, no matter how strong the impact of ceramic art was, the decisive role in Gauguin's creative evolution belonged to his own inborn inclinations which were awakened by his discovery of Martinique. A few months in Paris sufficed to reawaken Gauguin's irresistible urge to leave that city, and early in 1888 he again moved to Pont-Aven. Gauguin's break with this dualism and his turning to more essential and simpler elements devoid of any narrative overtones were largely influenced by Japanese art which he admired throughout his life. The Japanese print, with its flat forms, high horizon, asymmetrical composition and a well-defined outline dividing space into chromatically uniform planes, was a source of Gauguin's theoretical essays and practical experiments. One of the first paintings, which Gauguin himself links with his new aesthetics, is *Wrestling Boys* (private collection, Paris). The artist was not concerned with visual verisimilitude achieved through a precise rendition of every minute detail, for he firmly believed that true art could not exist without fantasy.

27. *Faaturama (Woman with a Red Dress or the Sulky Woman)*, 1891. Oil on canvas, 94.6 x 68.6 cm. Nelson-Atkins Museum of Art, Kansas City.

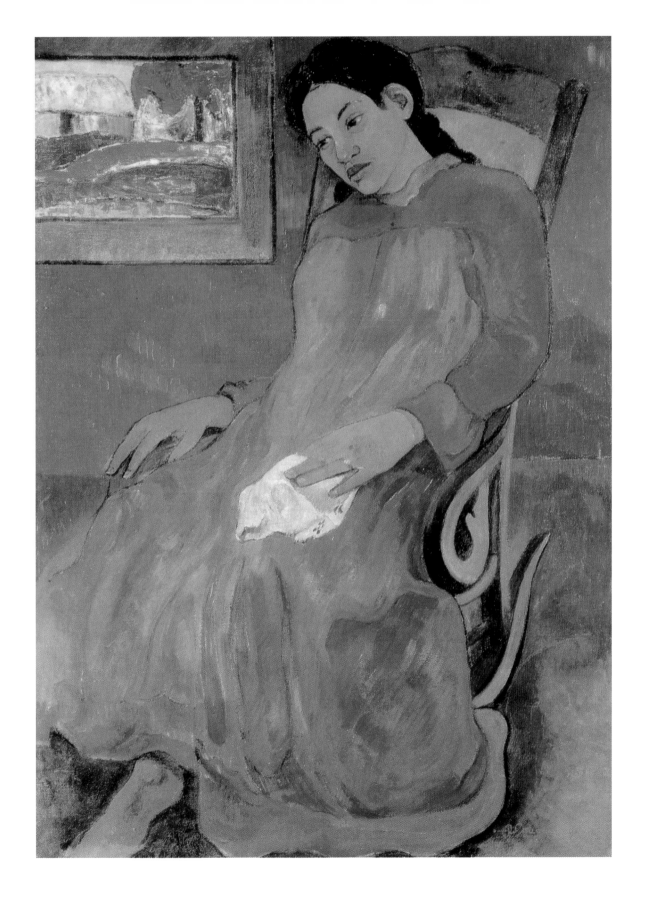

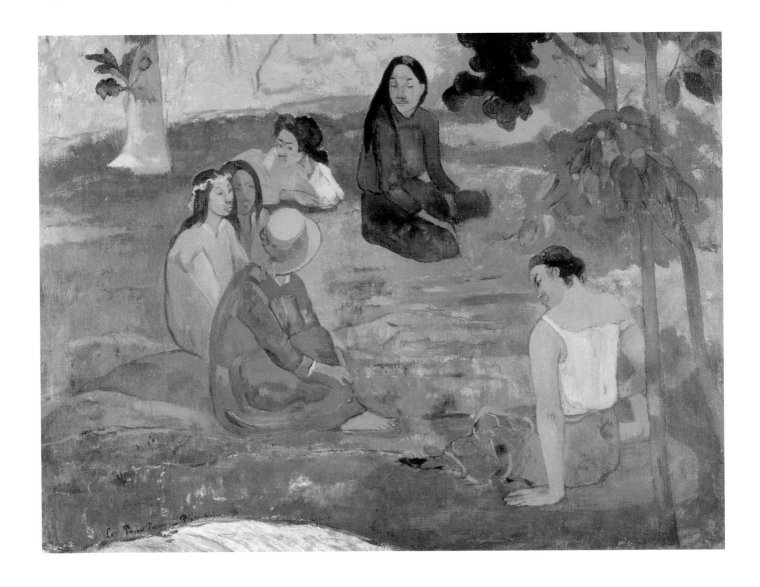

28. *The Parau Parau*
(Conversation), 1891.
Oil on canvas (relined),
71 x 92.5 cm.
The Hermitage,
St. Petersburg.

And he repeatedly expressed this view in conversations and letters. In 1888, he wrote to Schuffenecker: "A word of advice: don't paint too much direct from nature. Art is an abstraction, derive this abstraction from nature while dreaming before it, and think more of the creation that will result [8]". As a matter of fact, these ideas began to preoccupy Gauguin three years earlier.

Nowadays the majority of scholars agree that the indisputable leader of the Pont-Aven school was Gauguin, although Bernard certainly made his contribution – if not in painting proper, then in the theory of the trend. At the same time, most art historians still believe that Gauguin conceived the key work of the new trend, *The Vision after the Sermon*, or *Jacob Wrestling with the Angel* (National Gallery of Scotland, Edinburgh), under

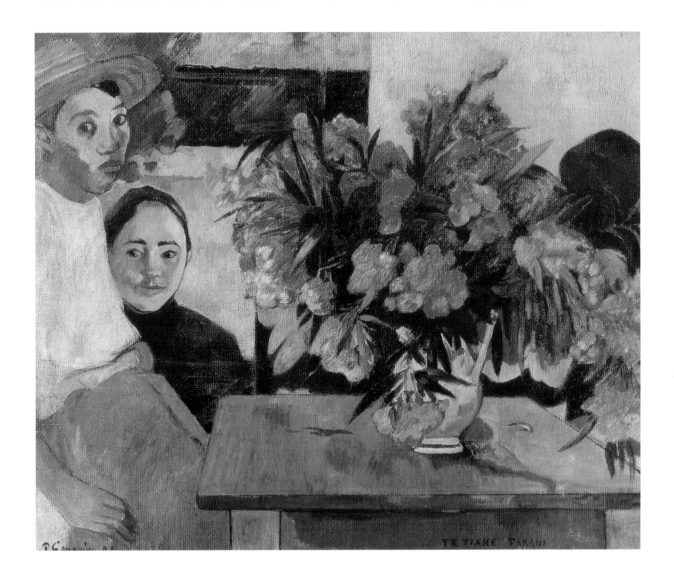

the influence of the *Breton Women in the Meadow* by Bernard (D. Denis collection, Saint-Germain-en-Laye). It is true that Gauguin's vision appeared after *Breton Women*, but this does not necessarily imply (as was convincingly shown by Mark Roskill) that he was influenced by Bernard's picture, for the general tendency of Gauguin's creative evolution and some of his previous works indicated a new artistic outlook and a realization of this in his painting.

Thus, having long sensed the conflict between the Impressionist outlook and his own, he gradually arrived at a strikingly precise formula: "For them there is no such thing as a landscape that has been dreamed, created from nothing. They focused their efforts around the eye, not on the mysterious centre of thought [9]".

29. *Te tiare farani* (*The Flowers of France*), 1891. Oil on canvas, 72 x 92 cm. The Pushkin Museum of Fine Arts, Moscow.

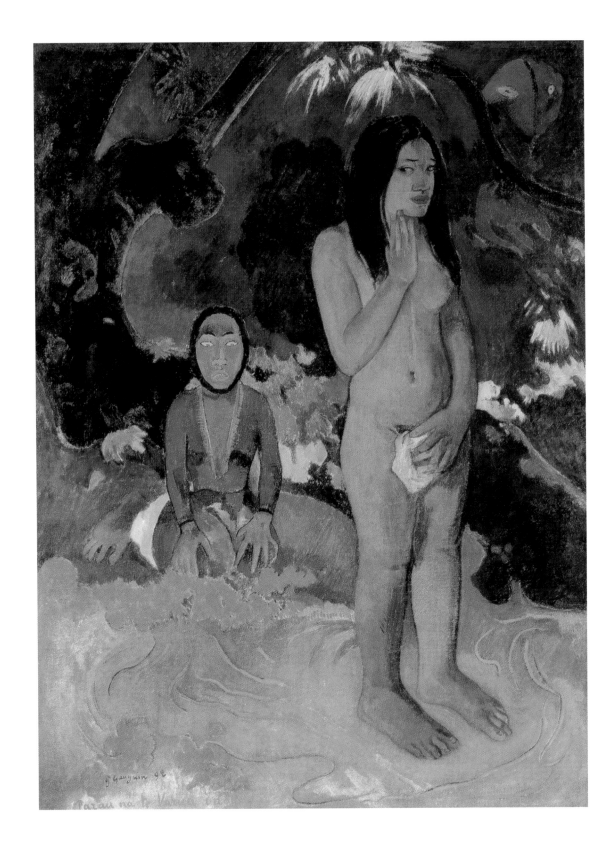

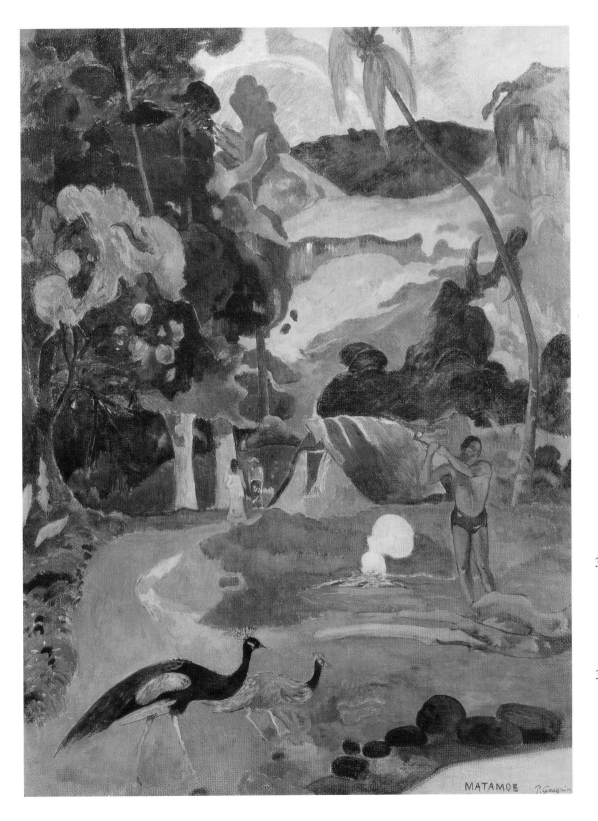

MATAMOE P.Gauguin

30. *Parau na te varua ino
(Evil's Words)*, 1892.
Oil on canvas,
91.7 x 68.5 cm.
National Gallery of
Art, Washington.

31. *Matamoe, Landscape
with Peacocks*, 1892.
Oil on canvas,
115 x 86 cm.
The Pushkin Museum
of Fine Arts, Moscow.

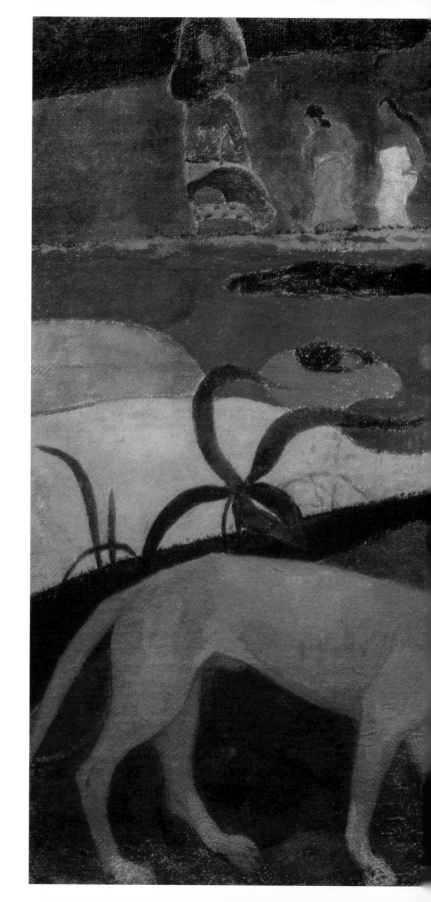

32. *Arearea (Happiness)*,
1892. Oil on canvas,
75 x 94 cm.
Musée d'Orsay, Paris.

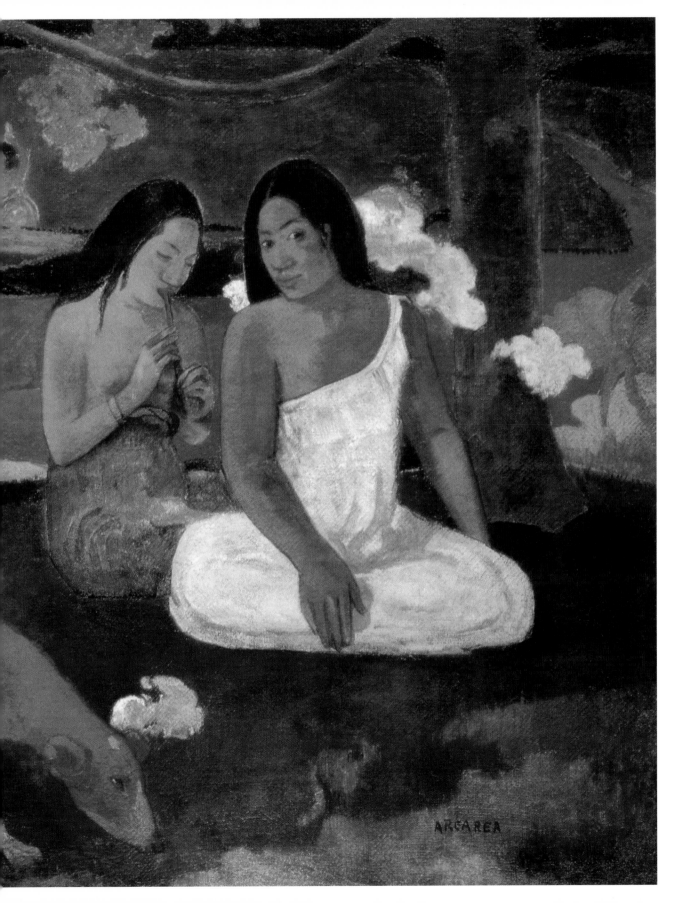

He was not satisfied with painting from life and recording visual experiences; yet life and nature were something he could not do without, for they inspired his dreams and fantasies, nourishing his imagination. He passed phenomena of life through the prism of his artistic vision and they re-emerged in a concentrated, generalized form. Hence the replacement of concrete individual images with the synthetic ones, bearing the eternal truth and recreating the mysterious past, the childhood of mankind – that is, all that was to become his major theme, particularly after his escape from Europe. This view on the essence of painting presupposed the artist's right to transform life with the help of emphatic linear treatment and expressive, strongly suggestive colouring so as to capture its intrinsic harmony and rhythm.

The Breton period was interrupted by a two-month visit to Arles, where he was invited by Van Gogh who looked forward to founding a kind of 'Workshop of the South' (L'Atelier du Midi) modelled on a medieval guild, in which like-minded artists could work together along new lines. The idea was doomed to failure, for Gauguin was the only painter who joined Van Gogh, and mainly because he hoped Vincent's brother Theo might help him escape from his poverty.

However dramatic their life together turned out to be, this period of intimate artistic communion had a profound significance for the work of both Gauguin and Van Gogh. Working side by side, each eager to prove he was right, they tried to re-examine a number of important questions. Perhaps it was in Arles that Gauguin finally saw what Japanese engraving could offer to his theory of synthesis. In any case, his attitude towards the treatment of light and shade, one of the basic means of reproducing reality in traditional European painting, came from the southern city.

During the two months when Van Gogh and Gauguin were in daily contact, the impact of their work was felt – both directly and indirectly – in the mutual borrowing of certain stylistic features and, even more so, in mutual differences. At times Gauguin and Van Gogh turned to the same subject, at which point the difference in their interpretation of visual experiences became even more apparent. Such are Gauguin's *Old Women of Arles* (Art Institute of Chicago) and Van Gogh's *Ladies of Arles* (Reminiscence of the Garden at Etten, Hermitage, St. Petersburg). Gauguin knew what he meant when he wrote that the women of Arles, "with their shawls, falling in folds, are like the primitives, like Greek friezes". He treats the figures and the landscape in a very economic manner, simplifying and generalizing forms and transforming volumes into flat silhouettes defined by near geometric contours and local colour. Van Gogh's picture, on the other hand, has nothing of the decorativeness of Gauguin's composition, with its mournful procession of women passing through a hospital garden and its undisturbed equilibrium of forms.

33. *Vaïraumati tei oa*
(Her Name is Vaïraumati), 1892.
Oil on canvas,
91 x 60 cm.
The Pushkin Museum of Fine Arts, Moscow.

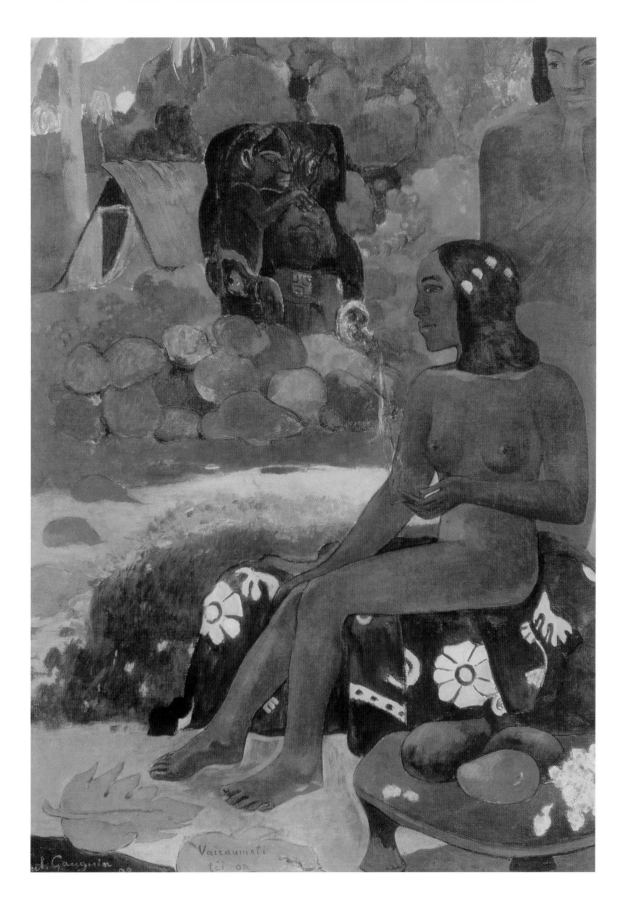

43

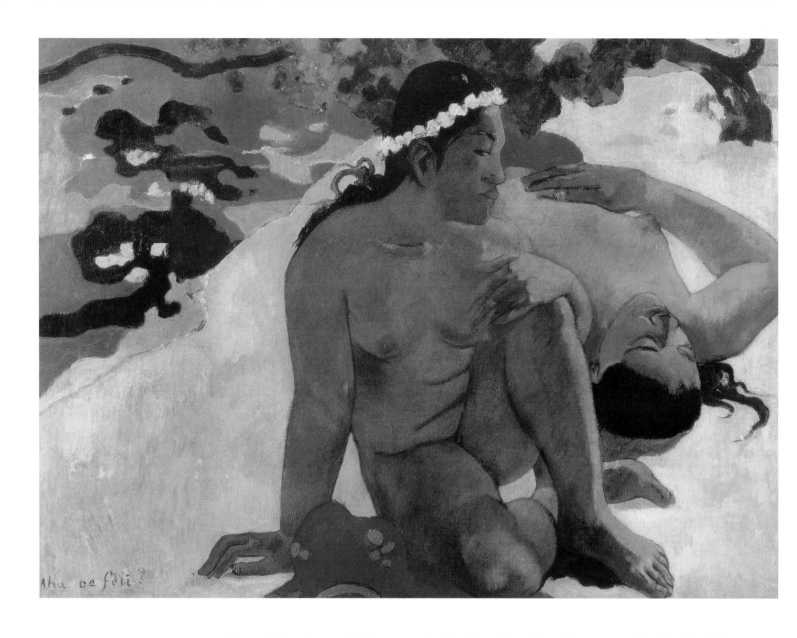

34. *Aha oe feii?* (*What!*
Are You Jealous?),
1892. Oil on canvas,
66 x 89 cm.
The Pushkin Museum
of Fine Arts, Moscow.

Gauguin's sojourn at Arles was cut off rather abruptly and unexpectedly. Van Gogh's extreme excitability and recurrent depressions turned the life of the two artists into a series of violent arguments and subsequent reconciliations. Van Gogh's attempt at suicide put an end to Gauguin's stay at his house. As soon as Theo had arrived at Arles and arranged for his brother to go into an asylum at his own request, Gauguin left for Paris. Finding himself back in the capital without funds, while waiting for the results of the Brussels exhibition (held in February-March 1889) Gauguin organized an exhibition of like-minded artists which took place in the Café Volpini in March and April that year.

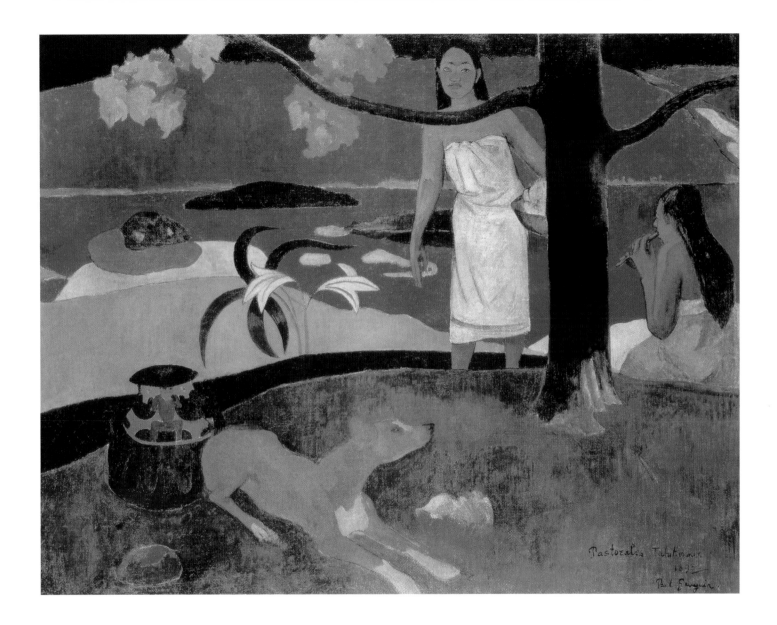

On his return to Paris, however, Gauguin felt a new strength welling up inside him. While still in Arles, he had written that he was as yet involved in a minor artistic skirmish, but was preparing for a great battle. "I want to go onto the attack only when I have all the necessary material in my hands [10]".

By 1889 all the preconditions for the "great battle" had been fulfilled. Having spent two months in Paris, Gauguin again left for Brittany, first to Pont-Aven and then to Le Pouldu, a small fishing village, where he rented a house together with his new friend and pupil Meyer de Haan.

35. *Pastorales tahitiennes*, 1893. Oil on canvas, 86 x 113 cm. The Hermitage, St. Petersburg.

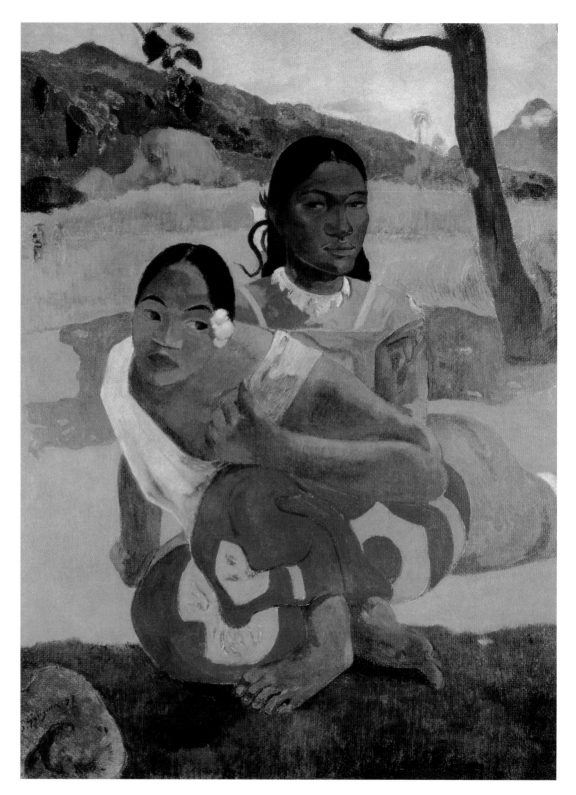

36. *Nafae faa ipopo?*
   When will you
   Marry? 1882.
   Oil on canvas,
   105 x 77.5 cm. Rudolf
   Staechelin Foundation.

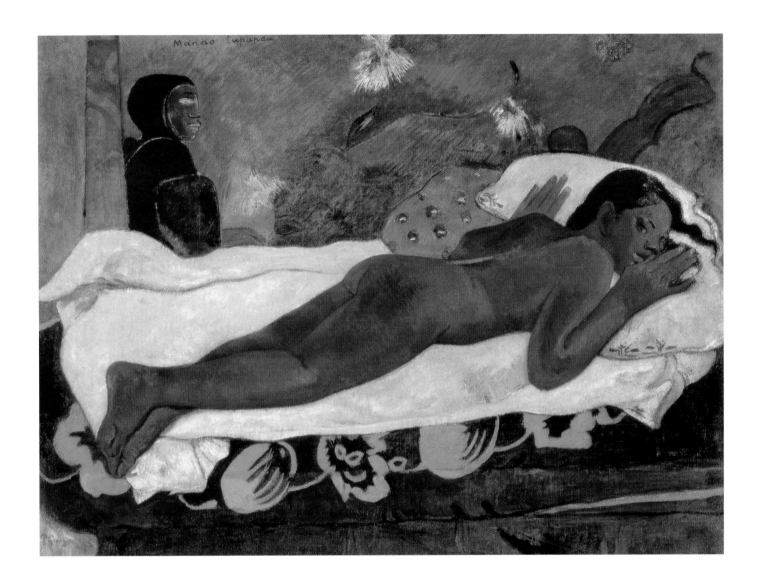

This time he began to see Brittany – its landscapes and colours – in a new light. Dull and uninspiring in winter, it was magically transformed by the summer and autumn sun. Yellow became Gauguin's favourite colour, dominating the palette of many of his Breton pictures, joyous and radiant as never before. Such are his *Haymaking in Brittany* (Courtauld Institute Galleries, London), *The Yellow Haystacks*, or *The Golden Harvest* (Musée d'Orsay, Paris), *The Brittany Landscape* (Nationalmuseum, Stockholm), two landscapes (Nasjonalgalleriet, Oslo), *The Yellow Christ* (Albright-Knox Art Gallery, Buffalo) and many other compositions. Yellow was the dominant colour, others – red, dark blue and purple, applied in broad sweeping strokes – were subservient to it. Used in various combinations, it determined the emotional key of the picture.

37. ***Manao Tupapau*** *(the Soul of the Dead Ones is Awake)*, 1892. Oil on canvas, 73 x 92 cm. Albright-Knox Art Gallery, Buffalo.

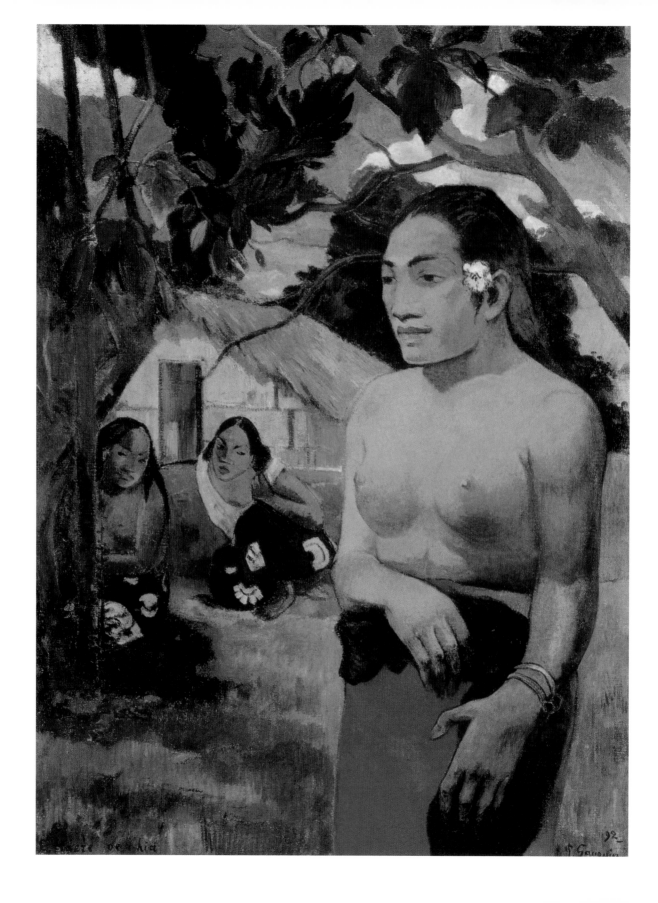

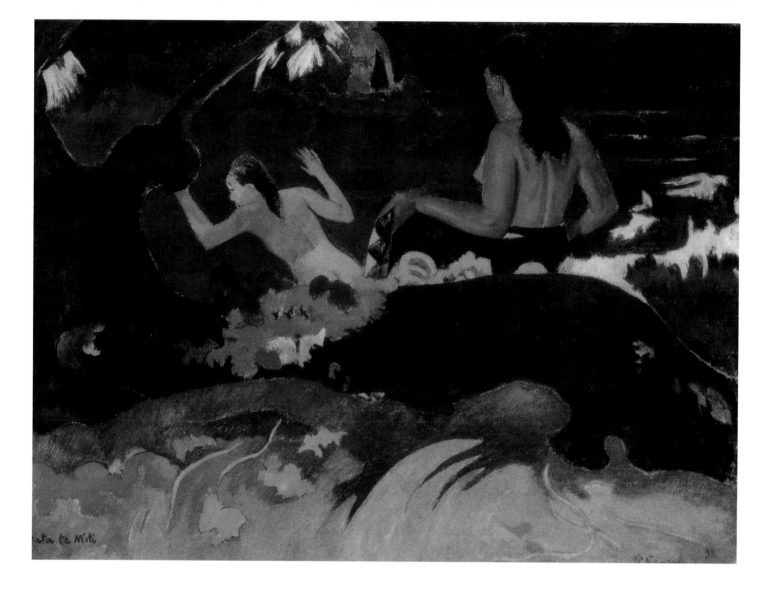

The style of these paintings already bore some features, which were to develop later, during Gauguin's Polynesian period.

And it was in this same light that Gauguin saw Breton fishermen, peasants and their children; to him they were also left aside by society, which hurried on with its cultural development. He painted them in a manner rejecting the deceptively flattering veil of the plein-air technique. But the savage primitiveness of Brittany was gradually losing its appeal for Gauguin. His poverty and the humiliating dependence upon his friends support made life unbearable. During his visits to Paris from Brittany Gauguin was a frequent guest at the literary clubs of the Symbolists.

38. *E haere oe I hia? Where are You Going?* 1892. Oil on canvas, 96 x 69 cm. Staatsgalerie, Stuttgart.

39. *Fatata te miti (On the Seashore)*, 1892. Oil on canvas, 68 x 92 cm. National Gallery, London.

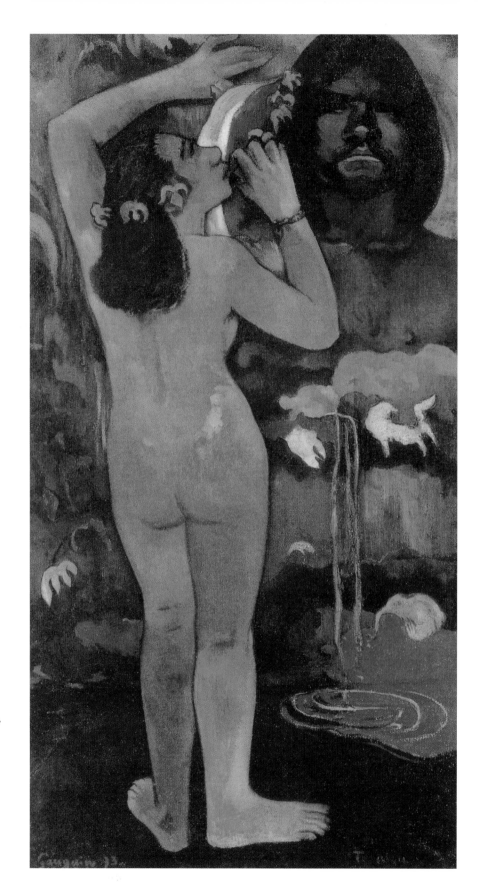

40. *Hina Tefatou (The Moon and the Earth)*, 1893. Oil on canvas, 112 x 62 cm. Museum of Modern Art, New York.

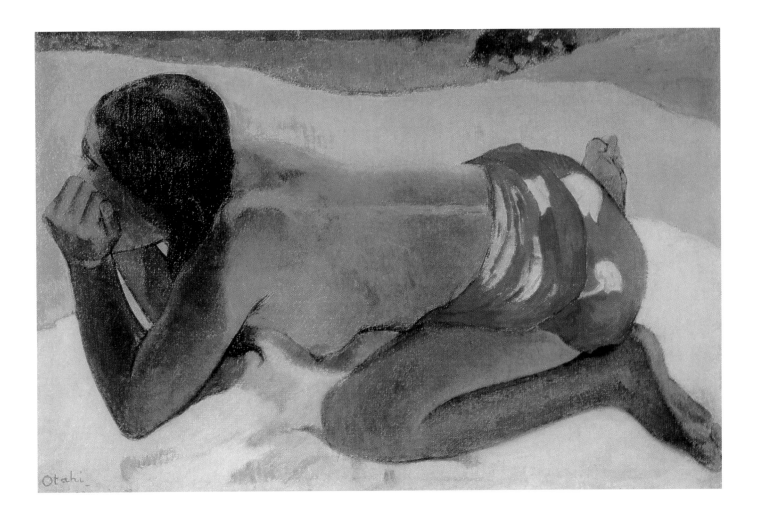

His meetings with the leading Symbolist poets, critics and theorists – Mallarmé, Mirbeau, Moréas, Aurier and Morice – and his participation in their literary discussions were a stimulating experience. At the same time, Gauguin was put on his guard, as it were, by the Symbolist literary aesthetics, and by the refinement of Parisian poets whose acute resentment of naturalism had led them away from reality and into an artificial imaginary world. The emotional and spiritual depth of Gauguin's works, combined with their decorativeness and monumentality of forms, induced Albert Aurier, a young poet and an ardent exponent of Symbolism, to hail Gauguin as the head of the Symbolist movement in art. The dream of a land caressed by a generous sun, of a land where the primitive is a natural phenomenon and not something imposed through historical and literary reminiscences, became almost an obsession.

41. *Otahi* (*Alone*), 1893.
Oil on canvas,
50 x 73 cm.
Private Collection.

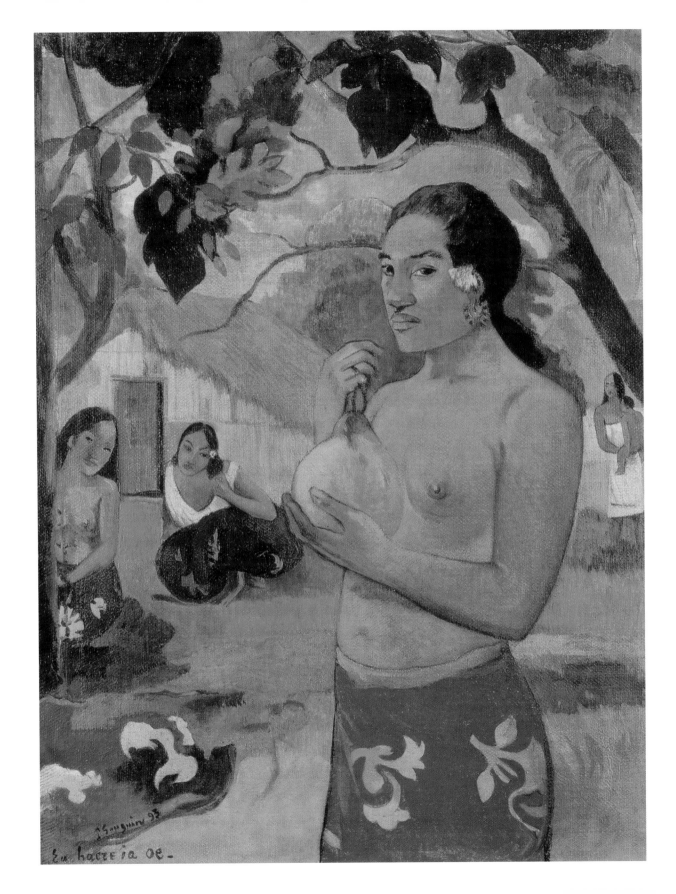

During the World Fair of 1889 in Paris, Gauguin was a constant visitor to the African, Javanese and Polynesian pavilions.

Indochina, Japan, Madagascar or Tahiti – in short, everything that was not Europe and that was not touched by bourgeois relationships – they all equally attracted Gauguin. "All the Orient – the great thought written with the golden letters in all their art; it's all worth studying. And it seems to me that I'll reimmerse myself there," he wrote when the decision to leave France had already been made. "The Occident is corrupt now, and all that is powerful can like Antaeus, renew its strength by touching the earth there ⁱ". Preparing for his departure, the artist collected the necessary materials – photographs of monuments of oriental art, reproductions, books, magazines and guidebooks. A new motif appeared in his works: a naked woman with the facial features of his mother, among tropical vegetation. Such was his *Exotic Eve* (private collection, Paris), an antipode of the two versions of the sorrowful *Breton Eve* (private collection, New York; Marion Koegler McNay Art Institute, San Antonio) painted only a year earlier. That exotic Eve was a link between his former style of the Martinique period and his future Tahitian one.

Having discussed his possible destination with his friends and rejected the idea of going to Tonking or Madagascar, Gauguin finally decided on Tahiti. An attempt to get an appointment as a governmental official that would provide him with a living proved hopeless, and in order to raise money for his voyage and settlement, in February 1891 Gauguin announced a sale of his works. After that he paid a short visit to his family in Copenhagen.

He was beginning to believe in his future fame, financial independence and, as a natural consequence, reunion with his family. At last, after a banquet in his honour given by his friends the Symbolists, Gauguin left for Tahiti in April 1891. He went alone, for none of his friends who had originally intended to go with him, ventured the voyage.

But Gauguin was not discouraged by the prospect of solitude. Strange as it may seem, he possessed two mutually exclusive qualities – a sober mind and incredible naivety. Leaving Europe he had visions of the harmonious and happy life of the Polynesians among whom he would find peace of mind and an opportunity to work to his heart's content.

The European world with its bourgeois conventions which had given birth to an insipid, uninventive art and which blocked the way for anything that was alive was too narrow for his romantic dream. "The terrible thirst for the unknown makes me commit follies," he confessed when he had just returned from Arles "hope that you will see an almost new Gauguin: I say 'almost' because I don't claim to invent something entirely new.

42. *Eu haere ia oe, Where are You Going? (Woman Holding a Fruit)*, 1893. Oil on canvas, 92 x 73 cm (relined), The Hermitage, St. Petersburg.

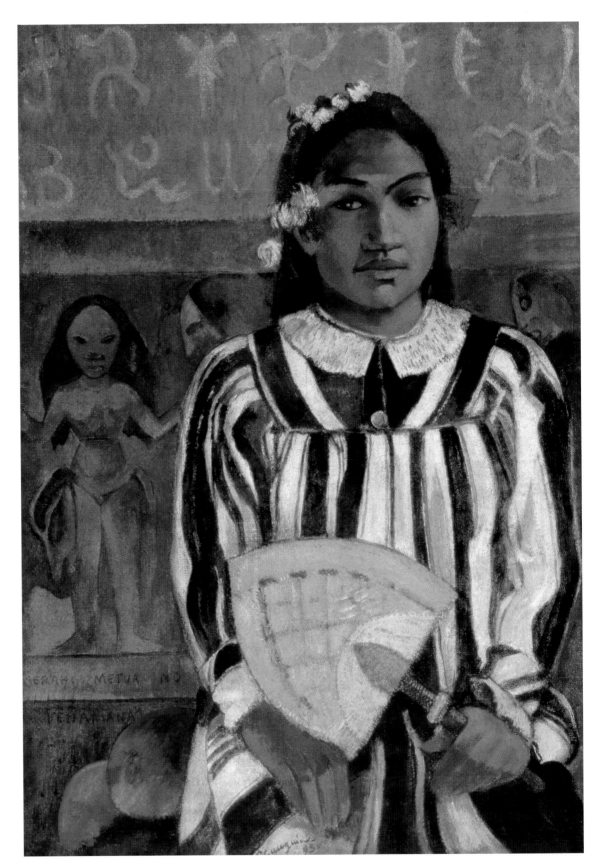

43. **Merahi metua no Tehamana**
   (Teha'mana Has many Parents), 1893.
   Oil on canvas,
   76 x 52 cm. Art
   Institute, Chicago.

44. **Self-Portrait with a Hat**, winter 1893-1894.
   Oil on canvas,
   46 x 38 cm.
   Musée d'Orsay, Paris.

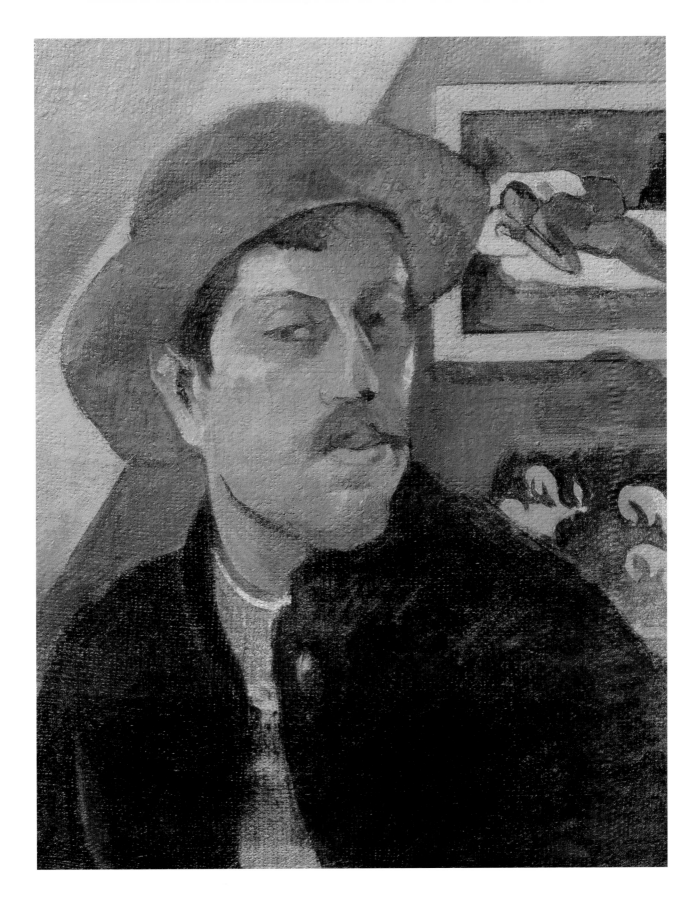

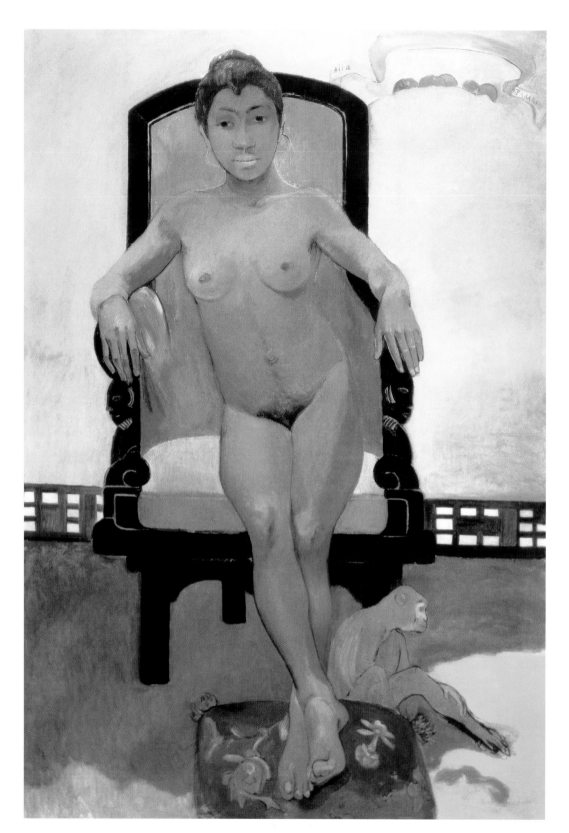

45. **Aita tamari vahine Judith te parari** *(Annah, the Javanese)*, 1893-1894. Oil on canvas, 116 x 81 cm. Private Collection.

46. **Self-Portrait with a Palette**, ca. 1894. Oil on canvas, 92 x 73 cm. Private Collection.

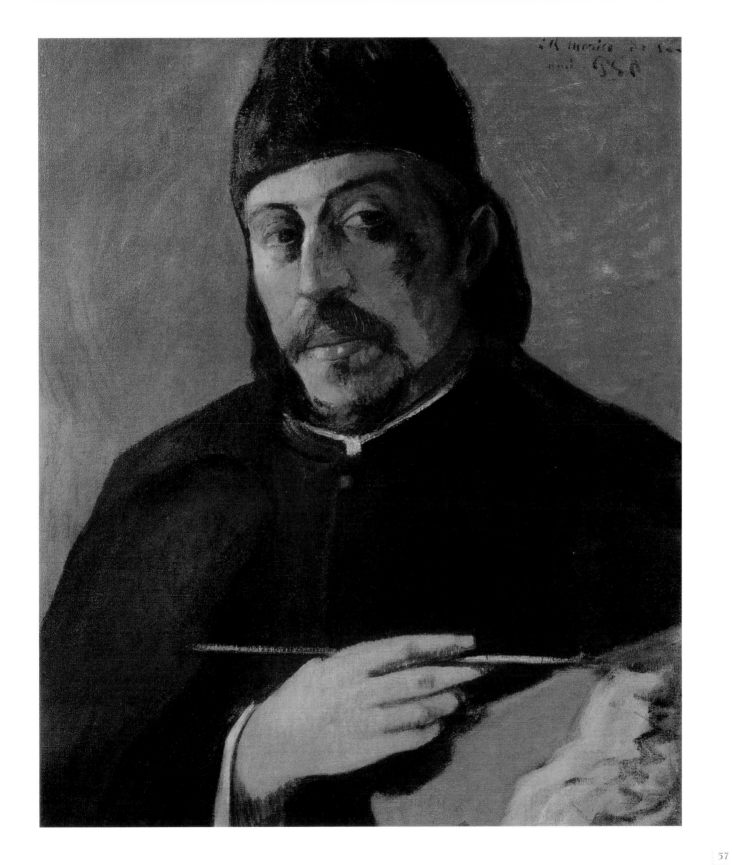

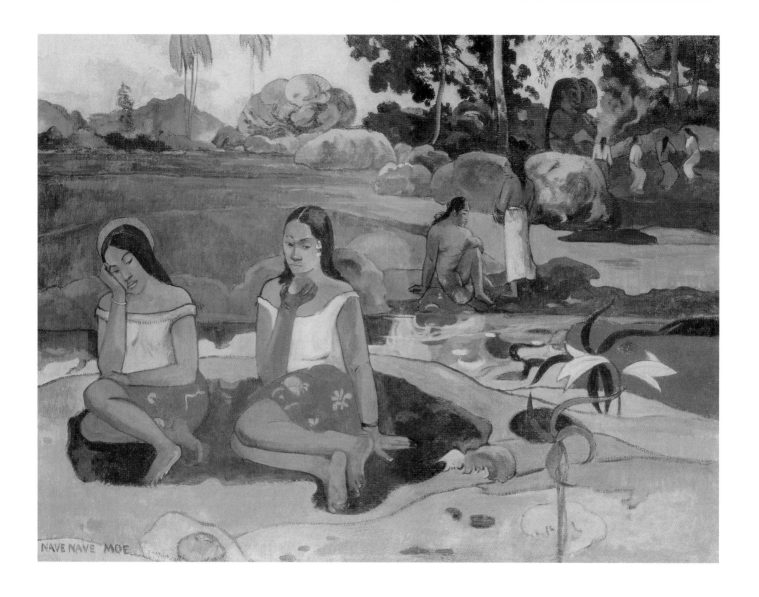

47. *Nave nave moe.*
Sacred Spring (or
Sweet Dreams), 1894.
Oil on canvas,
73 x 98 cm.
The Hermitage,
St. Petersburg.

I only wish to discover in me an as yet unknown facet "[12] – these prophetic words were written by Gauguin two years before his voyage to Tahiti, when he couldn't yet know that his wish would come true there. In the early morning of 8 June 1891, after sixty-three days at sea in forced idleness and feverish anticipation of a meeting with his future, Gauguin set foot on the soil of Noa Noa. The day before he had celebrated his forty-third birthday. His first contact with Tahitian reality showed that Papeete was by no means paradise, that civilization – in the person of officials, traders and soldiers – had long since firmly established itself in this colonial capital of the island. He realized that the childhood of mankind, the idyllic past in which man was an integral part of

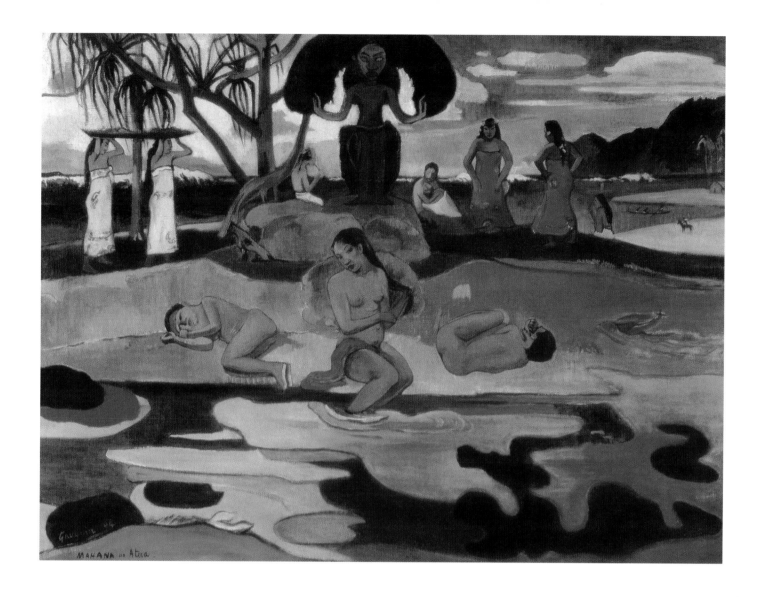

nature, in quest of which he had left Europe, had to be sought outside the city here, too. Nothing in Papeete, nor any of his fellow-passengers on the voyage inspired him to a picture. He hastened away from the capital and settled on the southern coast of Tahiti, at Mataiea, in one of the houses between the sea and a hill with a deep cleft overgrown by mango-trees. Enchanted with the bright colours of the sea and of the coral reefs, surrendering himself to the slow rhythm of Tahitian life, the artist imbibed and accumulated his new visual experiences. He drew a series of studies from nature, sketched characteristic poses, faces and groups of figures. One of the first portraits painted in Tahiti was *Woman with a Flower* (Ny Carlsberg Glyptotek, Copenhagen).

48. *Mahana no atua*
   (The Day of the God),
   1894. Oil on canvas,
   68.3 x 91.5 cm. Art
   Institute, Chicago.

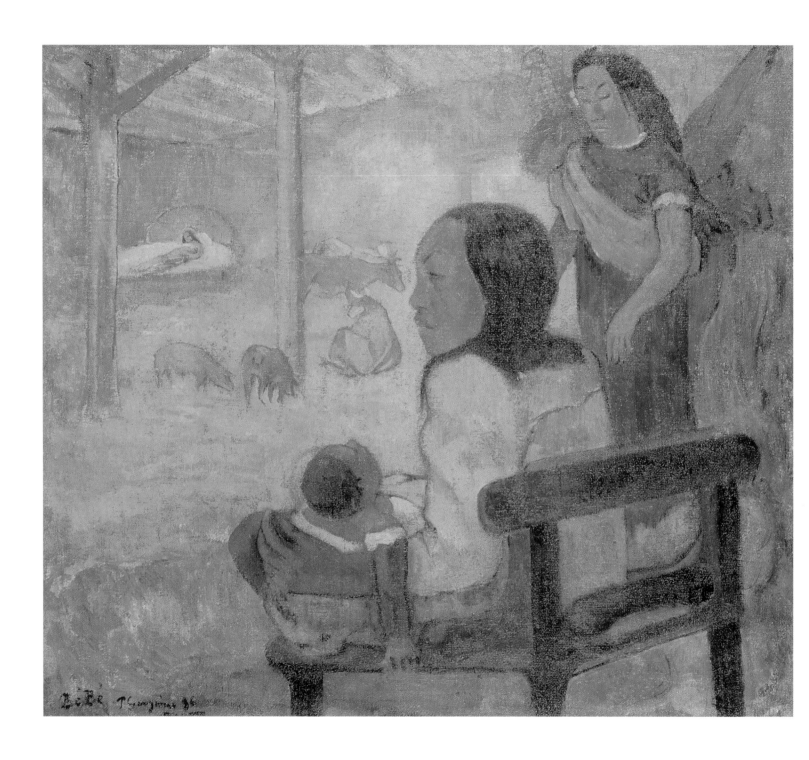

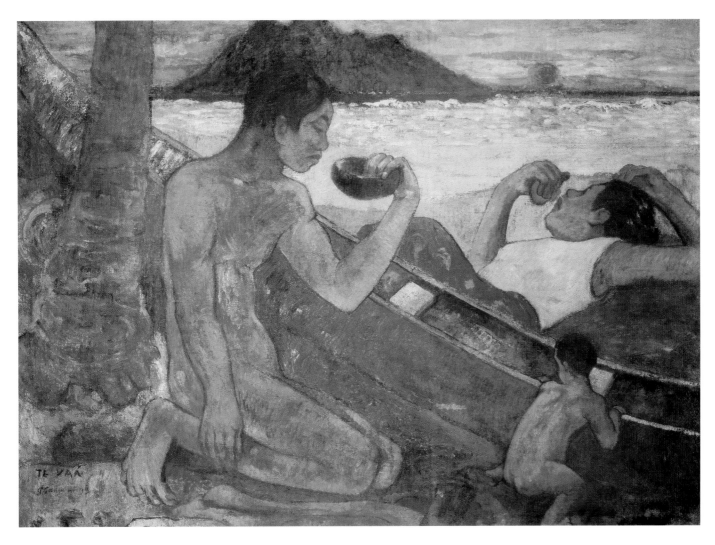

Although both the artist and the model seem to have felt a certain constraint, the portrait is remarkable for its monumental simplicity. The arrangement of the figure on the surface, the subtle modelling of the head and face, and the colouring all bespeak the artist's integral perception of the model and her character. Oceanian nature almost at once enriched Gauguin's palette and called new plastic forms into being, although it was only eleven months after his arrival to Tahiti that he ventured to say that he had acquired a feel of Tahitian soil and its fragrance. At Mataiea Gauguin also painted his first Tahitian landscapes, to which belongs *At the Foot of a Mountain* (Hermitage, St. Petersburg), Where the tiny figure of a horseman emphasizes the magnificence of nature.

49. *Bé Bé, the Nativity*, 1896. Oil on canvas, 66 x 75 cm. The Hermitage, St. Petersburg.

50. *Te vaa, The Canoe* (*a Tahitian Family*) 1896. Oil on canvas, 96 x 130.5 cm. The Hermitage, St. Petersburg.

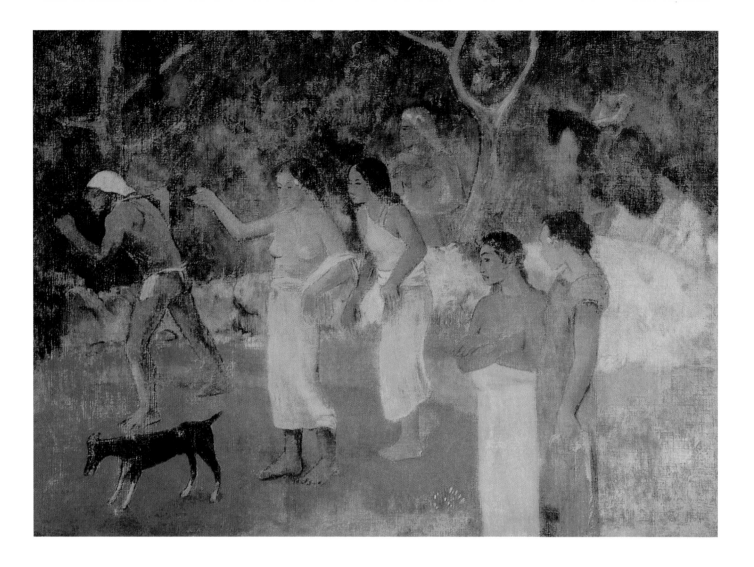

51. *Scene from Tahitian Life*, 1896.
Oil on canvas,
89 x 125 cm.
The Hermitage,
St. Petersburg.

**52. *Eiaha Ohipa*
(*Tahitians in a Room*),**
1896. Oil on canvas,
65 x 75 cm.
The Pushkin Museum
of Fine Arts, Moscow.

In a number of pictures of this period, the stylized effects of the cloisonnist technique are almost completely ousted by a softer and more natural treatment. The gently applied strokes of red paint against a large monochrome area of yellow in the foreground create the illusion of shadows gliding in the air and on the ground surface. The same broad, sweeping brushwork distinguishes another landscape, *The Big Tree* (Art Institute of Chicago). While discovering the beauty of the new land, the artist did not feel it necessary to modify his visual impressions, since both the landscape and the people in it were fairly exotic, mysterious and picturesque. That is why his early Tahitian works display a greater verisimilitude. This idea — the opposition of civilization and barbarism — which goes back to the European Romanticist tradition, acquired a special significance in Gauguin's art.

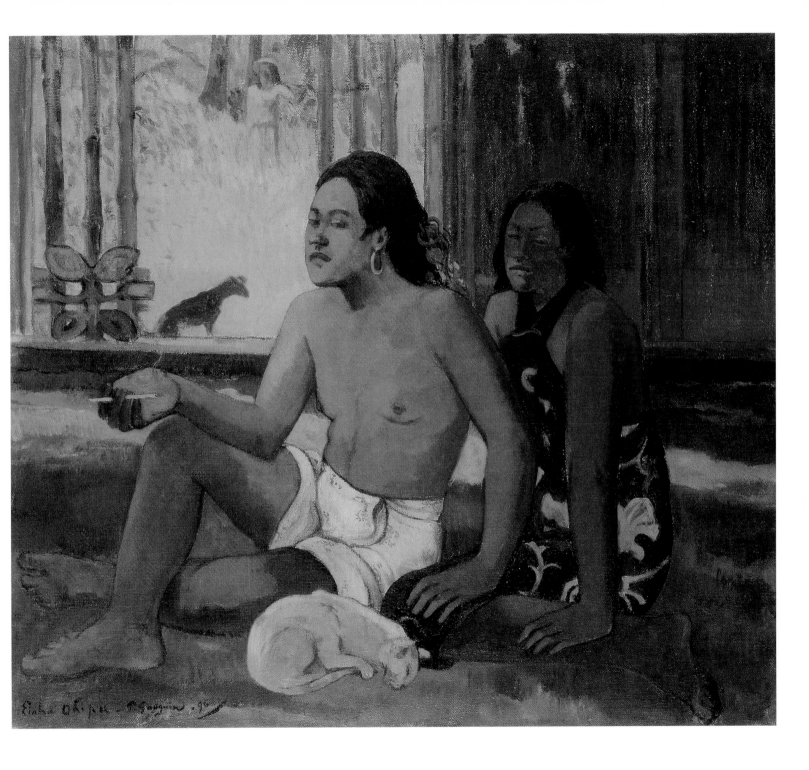

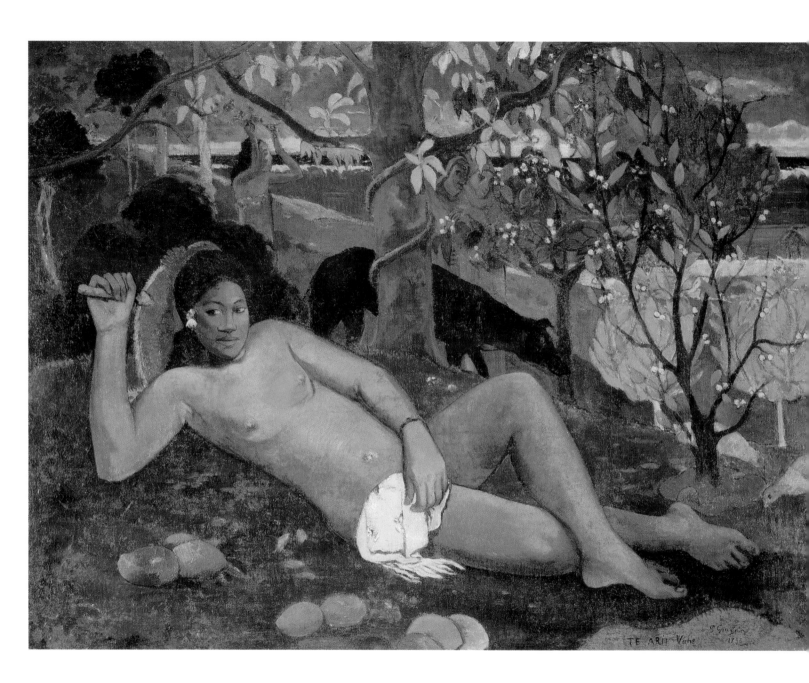

It formed the basis of his aesthetic conception and inspired his interest in the culture of primitive peoples long before his arrival in Oceania. This idea also underlies his book *Noa Noa* and directly relates to one of the episodes narrated in it.

From now on the artist could orchestrate his planes and surfaces with the boldest lines and arabesques. He could "lay on the canvas red, blue…all this gold, all this sunny joyfulness without a second thought…" [13]

In Tahiti Gauguin was reconsidering his attitude to Greek art, opposing it to archaic art which, in his view, possessed greater value, as it emerged from the people's creative imagination. "The animal substance that remains in all of us," Gauguin wrote from Oceania, "is not at all deserving of scorn as is usually supposed. It was those devilish Greeks who thought up Antaeus, gathering his strength from touching the earth. The earth — that is our animal substance [14]".

Most compositions are centred on one or two figures sitting, standing or lying down, with no narrative link between them. A case in point is - *What! Are You Jealous?* (Pushkin Museum, Moscow). Gauguin considered it (in August 1892) his most successful nude study. Sending it to the Copenhagen exhibition, he ranked it next in importance to his *Spirit of the Dead Watching* (Albright-Knox Art Gallery, Buffalo, New York; A. Conger Goodyear collection, 1965), which was particularly dear to his heart as a memento of Tehura, his Tahitian vahine.

The first thing that struck Gauguin in Tahiti was the statue-like immobility of the natives, who could sit or stand in one and the same position for hours on end. This ability of his models greatly appealed to the artist, for lack of movement in his pictures had long become a more or less consistent principle since the Pont-Aven period.

The new orientation of Gauguin's creative research is evident in his *Pastorales Tahitiennes* (Hermitage, St. Petersburg), *Amusements* (Musée d'Orsay, Paris) and *Autrefois* (private collection, New York). These works are not mere studies of Tahitian nature, but pictorial representations of the essence extracted from it and transformed by the artist's imagination. In the *Pastorales*, everything stands still, suggesting the enchanted world of reverie.

Paintings inspired by Polynesian legends occupy a special place in Gauguin's works. The lore and rituals of the Maori, already forgotten by Gauguin's contemporaries but recorded by Jacques-Antoine Moerenhout in an ethnographical study which fell into the artist's hands, nourished his imagination and enabled him to "rekindle a fire out of the ashes of the old furnace [15]".

Fruitful though this stay in Tahiti was, illness and constant lack of money eventually forced Gauguin to return to France, where he was as ever haunted by the image of his "promised land".

53. *Te Arii vahine, The king's Wife* (*The Queen*), 1896. Oil on canvas, 97 x 130 cm. The Pushkin Museum of Fine Arts, Moscow.

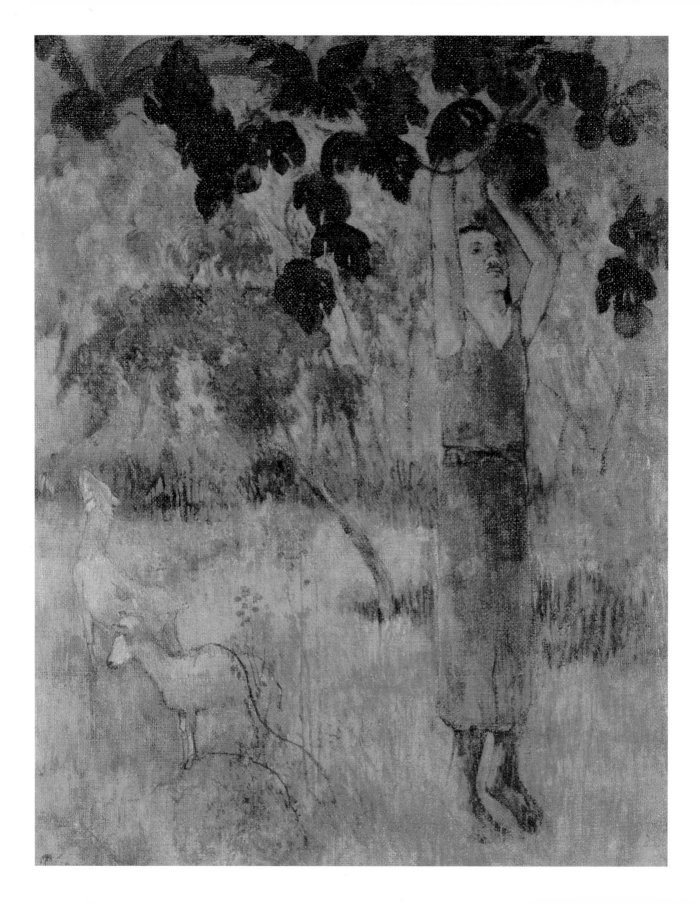

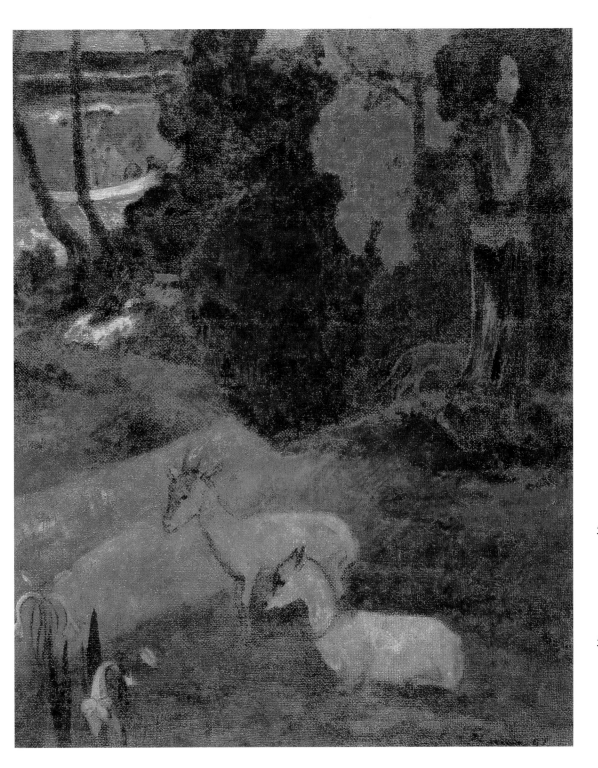

54. ***Man Picking Fruit from a Tree***, 1897.
Oil on canvas,
92 x 72 cm.
The Hermitage,
St. Petersburg.

55. ***Tarari Maruru, Landscape with two Goats***, 1897.
Oil on canvas,
93 x 73 cm.
The Hermitage,
St. Petersburg.

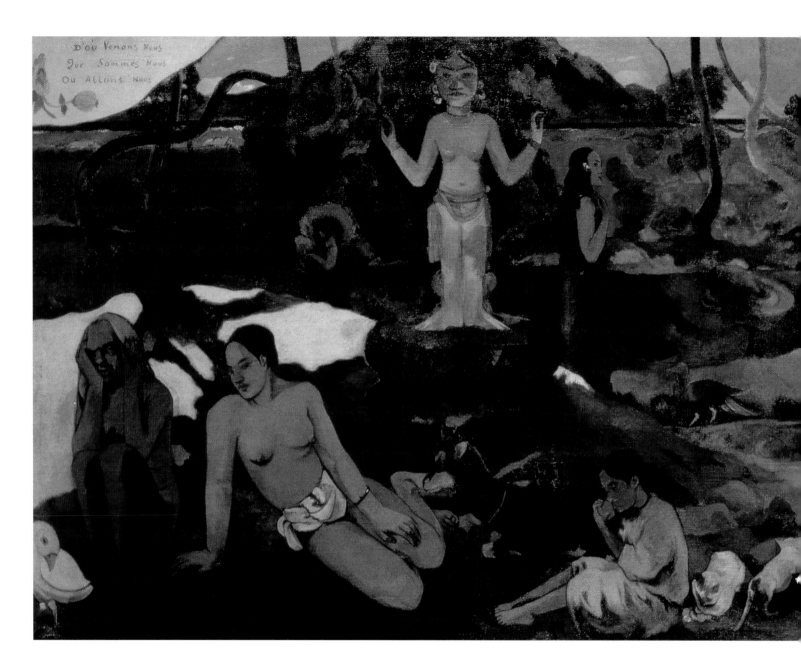

56. ***Where Do We Come
from? What are we?
Where are we Going?***
1897-1898. Oil on canvas,
139.1 x 374.6 cm.
Museum of Fine Arts,
Boston.

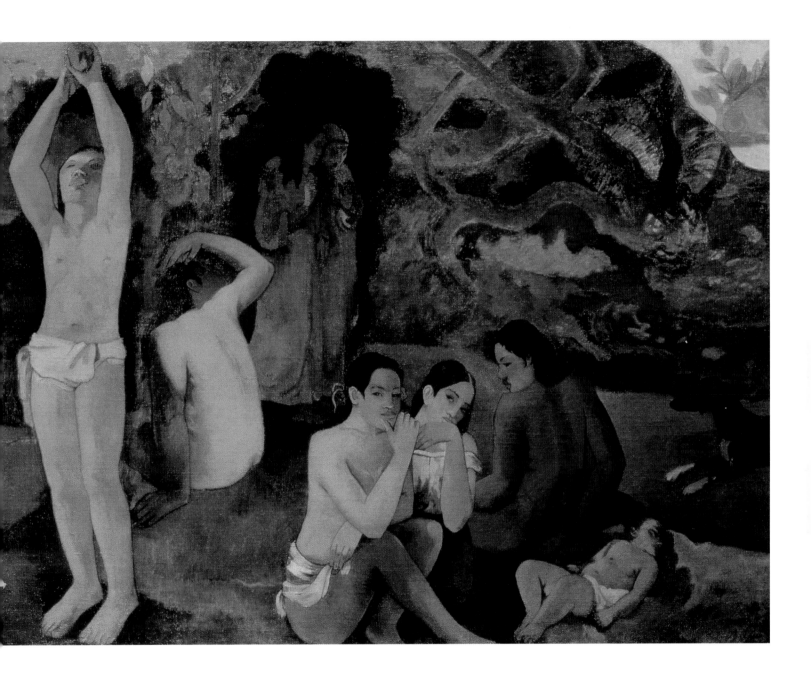

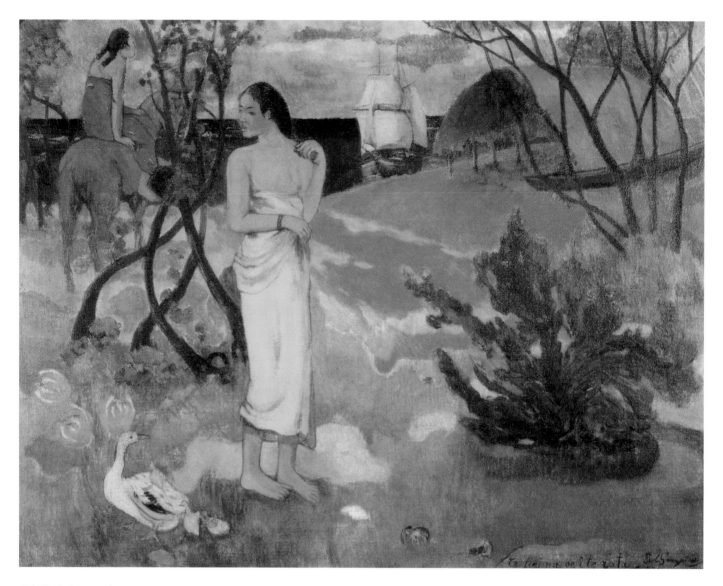

57. *Te tiai na oe ite rata*, *(Are You Waiting for a Letter?)*, 1899. Oil on canvas, 73 x 94 cm. Private Collection.

58. *Two Tahitians* *(Breast with Red Flowers)*, 1899. Oil on canvas, 94 x 72.2 cm. Metropolitan Museum of Art, New York.

In Paris he wrote *Noa Noa*, prepared drawings and prints for the text, and continued to paint on Tahitian motifs. His Paris canvases seem to be woven from memories of his recent past, as, for example, *Sacred Spring* (Hermitage, St. Petersburg) and *The Day of the God* (Art Institute of Chicago).

In France Gauguin was hounded by misfortune. His efforts to re-establish relations with his family came to nothing, while a trip to Brittany ended in tragedy: he broke his ankle and sustained a wound which never healed. But worst of all was the fact that the public and the critics did not accept his art.

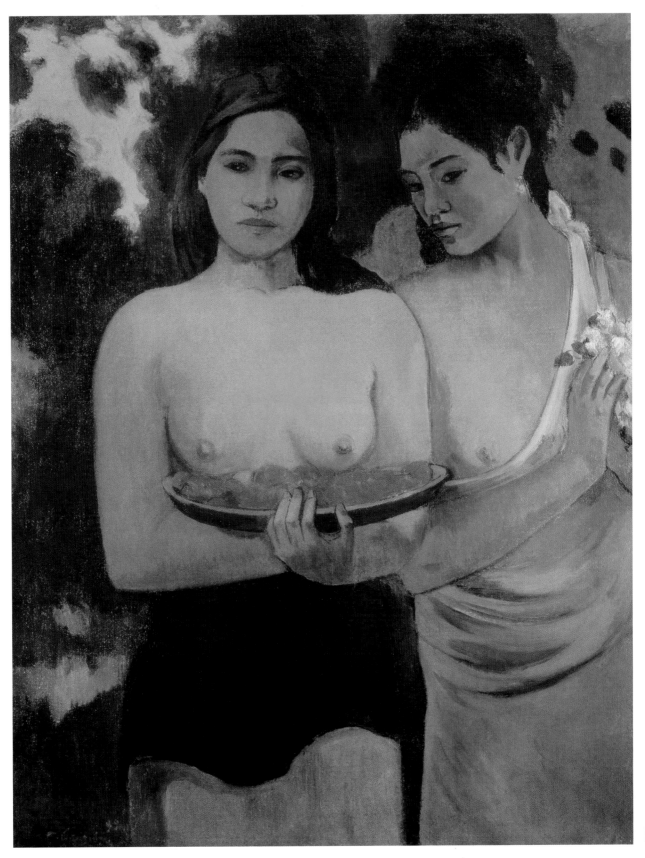

And soon, in the autumn of 1895, he again arrived in Tahiti. This time he settled on the west coast, at Punaauia, a small village near Papeete — the only place with a hospital and professional doctors, whose help Gauguin now needed almost daily. He built himself a bamboo cottage, and soon his new Tahitian vahine came to live with him. Very quickly he was again in desperate need of money. The futility and humiliation of his constant struggle for existence and the lost faith in his recognition as an artist made him think of committing a suicide.

But the vital force of his creative impulse was still very strong, and his desperate pessimism soon gave way to a new urge to work. His unfading admiration for the visual, sensual beauty of nature distracted him from his pains and troubles, and in the spring of 1896, when he was passing through a period of profound depression, he painted a series of brilliant works which opened his second Tahitian period. The highlight of this group of paintings is *The Queen* (Pushkin Museum, Moscow).

The Queen was the most perfect manifestation of his quest for primordial harmony. The artist repeated this composition with slight alterations and in different techniques several times — in a pen drawing, with watercolours and in woodcuts. Explaining his interpretation of this theme which recurs in numerous works executed in Tahiti, Gauguin wrote that he wanted to evoke through his picture of simple, naked nature the feeling of a pristine, barbaric luxury.

Gauguin's canvases of that period are peopled with static figures of Tahitian women absorbed in dreamy contemplation; they are depicted in isolation, in pairs or groups, in front of their huts or inside them. So are *The Dream* (Courtauld Institute Galleries, London), *Tahitians in a Room* (Pushkin Museum, Moscow), *The Canoe* (Hermitage, St. Petersburg) and its version *The Poor Fisherman* (São Paulo Museu de Arte), *Why Are You Angry?* (Art Institute of Chicago) and *Nevermore* (Courtauld Institute Galleries, London). Living in the South Pacific, Gauguin perceived oriental art not as a European admiring exotic curiosities, or as those artists who brought back from their travels wrestling scenes and various piquant subjects, or like Pierre Loti, a famous writer who looked down at Tahiti or Japan with an air of condescending superiority. For Gauguin, the art of the Orient was an integral part of his own aesthetic conception. His keen observation enabled him to discern essential similarities in various primitive cultures — Greece and Polynesia, Ancient Egypt and Japan, India and Cambodia, Italian primitive and medieval French artisans.

The life in Polynesia, where the natural world itself was full of mystic symbolism, and where the very existence of man — from birth to death — had a simpler, purer and more natural meaning, led to a further development of symbolist tendencies in Gauguin's art.

59. *Maternity* (*Women on the Seashore*), 1899. Oil on canvas (relined), 94 x 72 cm. The Hermitage, St. Petersburg.

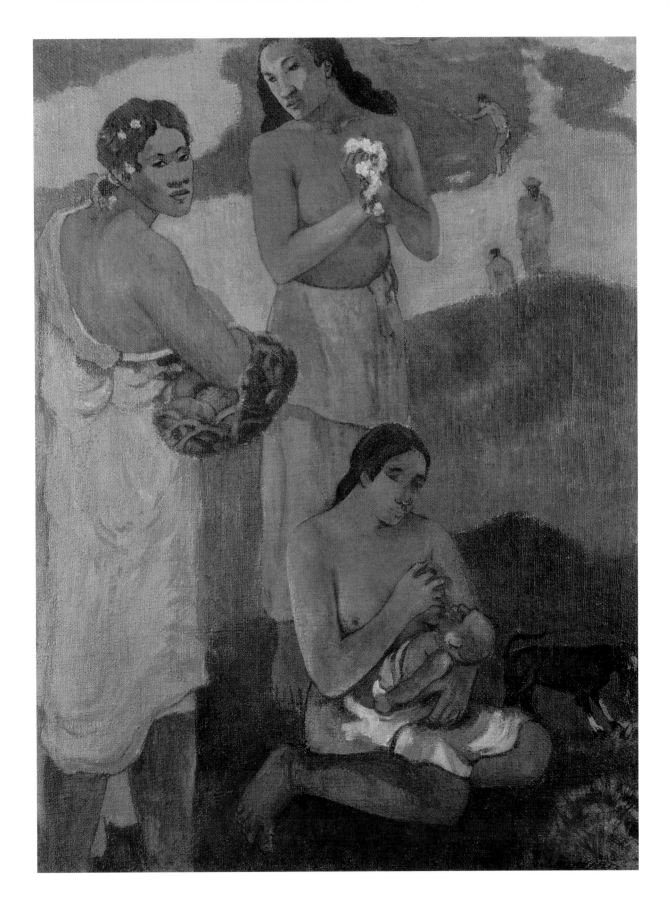

1897 is one of the unhappiest years in Gauguin's life. He received news of the death of his sixteen-year-old daughter, suffered unbearable physical pain and was subject to spells of blindness. Driven by all this to the point of committing suicide, he created his largest picture, *Where Do We Come From? What Are We? Where Are We Going?* (Museum of Fine Arts, Boston, USA), painted as his final statement. Two of the Hermitage works are related to this composition: *Landscape with Two Goats*, executed in a dark, sombre tonality, and *Man Picking Fruit from a Tree*, painted in a thin misty layer of ghostly yellow. The artist's return to life was marked by such works as *Preparations for a Feast* (Faa Iheihe) (Tate Gallery, London), *Gathering Fruit* (Pushkin Museum, Moscow), *Two Tahitian Women* (Metropolitan Museum of Art, New York), *Maternity*, *Woman Carrying Flowers* and *Three Tahitian Women against a Yellow Background*. Some of them are thematically or iconographically related to *Preparations for a Feast*, in which Gauguin returns to the motif of the Promised Land, using the specific set of pictorial devices.

A decorative pattern also appears in the Hermitage version of *Maternity*, but its function here is markedly different. The motif of a woman suckling her baby turns into a symbol of motherhood, of the great mystery of nature.

During this period Gauguin elaborated yet another theme, which had long preoccupied him — the theme of the common origin of different religions, particularly Buddhism and Christianity, to which he devoted a number of socio-theological writings and paintings, among them *The Last Supper* (Mme Katia Granoff collection, Paris) and *The Great Buddha* (Pushkin Museum, Moscow).

A burst of creative energy inspired Gauguin to undertake the last journey of his life, yet further into the heart of Polynesia, to the tiny island of Hivaoa in the Marquesas group. "Here poetry appears of its own accord, and when you paint you only have to abandon yourself to reverie to give expression to it. I only ask for two years of health, and not too many money worries, which now have an excessive hold on my nervous temperament, in order to reach a certain maturity in my art. I feel that I'm right about art — but will I have the strength to express it convincingly enough[16]", he wrote from his newly built "Maison du Jouir" at Atuona.

Fascinated by the wild, primitive beauty of nature, the artist pours out onto his works a joy that is almost painful in its intensity.

It is hard to believe, that such joyous paintings, as *Still Life with Parrots*, *The Ford* (both in the Pushkin Museum, Moscow), the two versions of *Riders on the Beach* (Folkwang, Museum, Essen; Stavros Niarchos collection, New York), and *Girl with a Fan* (Folkwang Museum, Essen), were done by a fatally ill man almost on the threshold of his death.

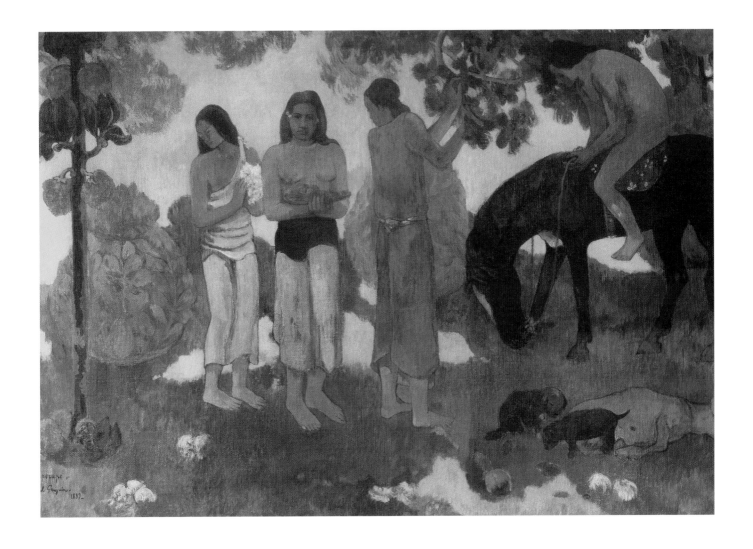

Fate gave Gauguin two years of life in Atuona, and despite his illness and his exasperating conflict with the colonial authorities, he still had enough strength to prove that "in his art he was right". His immersion in the depths of a different culture outside the European tradition gave his work a specific character which partly hid the true significance of his artistic aspirations in exotic, savage forms. Turning to the art of primitive and ancient peoples, to their folklore and crafts, Gauguin not only rescued from oblivion the poetic world of Oceanian culture and made its luxurious forms and colours accessible to us, but also enriched the artistic tradition of the West.

60. *Ruperupe (Gathering Fruit)*, 1899. Oil on canvas, 128 x 190 cm. The Pushkin Museum of Fine Arts, Moscow.

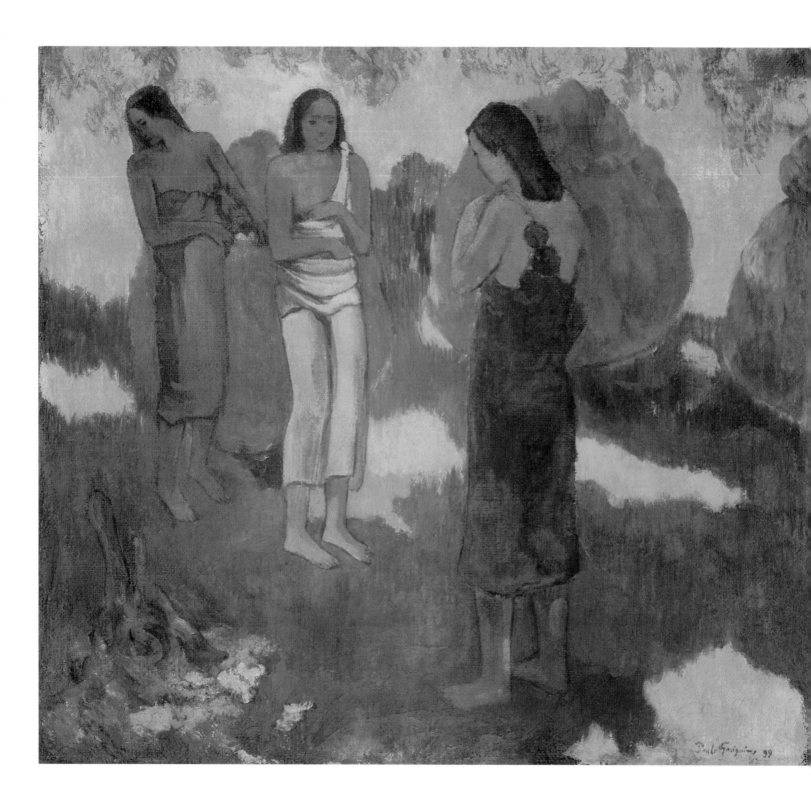

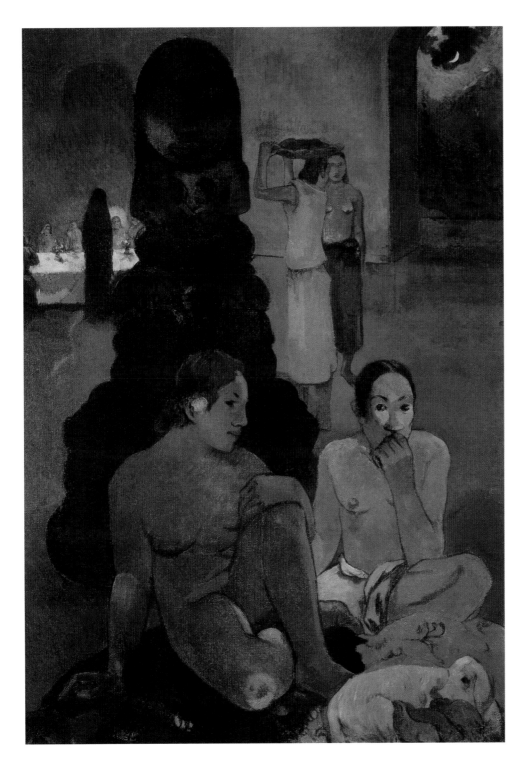

61. ***Three Tahitian
Women against a
Yellow Background***,
1899. Oil on canvas
(relined), 68 x 74 cm.
The Hermitage,
St. Petersburg.

62. ***The Great Buddha***
(The Idol), 1899.
Oil on canvas,
134 x 95 cm.
The Pushkin Museum
of Fine Arts, Moscow.

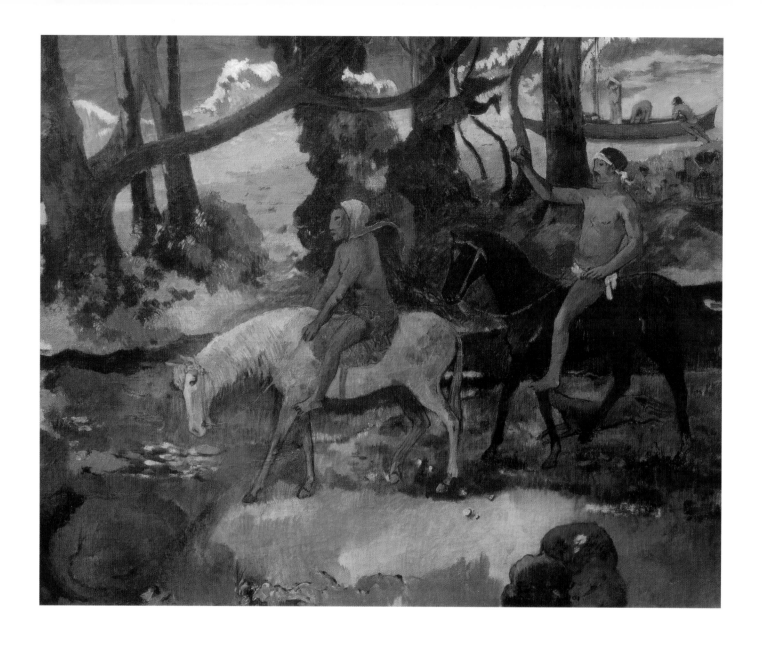

63. ***The Ford*** *(The Flight)*, 1901. Oil on canvas, 76 x 95 cm. The Pushkin Museum of Fine Arts, Moscow.

Gauguin belongs to those masters whose work marks a turning point in the history of art. In his quest of creating, and by no means imitating, the real world, he discovered its intrinsic fantastic elements and set new goals before art.

After Gauguin, interest in black art or the art of the Aztecs, Ancient Egypt or Japan became a matter of course. But Gauguin never imitated the external art forms of this or that people, or of this or that work by his contemporaries. He borrowed and absorbed only that which was in time with his own artistic and philosophic vision and which he

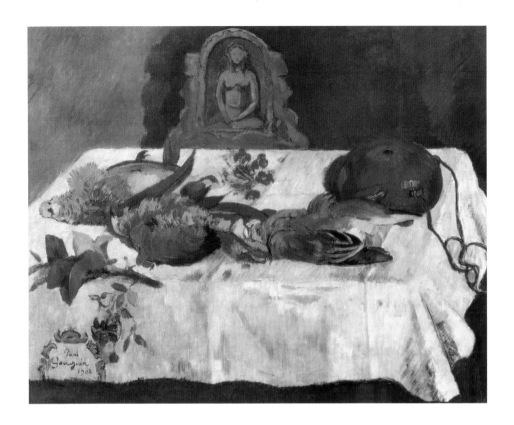

embodied in his work in a new original manner. His borrowings made local art part of world culture. The aspiration to record emotional and mental states not through the subject-matter, but with the help of plastic forms and colouring, led Gauguin beyond the boundaries of the classical artistic tradition which was considered the only correct and acceptable one in Europe. The simplification of form, the use of pure colour, the approach to colour as a pictorial equivalent of light, the arrangement of space by the juxtaposition of contrasting areas of colour, the right to construct a work according to his own independent artistic laws, the right to intervene actively in the visible world and by reshaping it to reveal some as yet unknown aspects of reality — in short, everything that lay at the source of modern art, if it did not find its systematic realization in Gauguin's works, was at least formulated by him on the level of artistic theory. His clear understanding of the creative tasks which the next generations were to resolve enables us to regard Gauguin as one of the immediate predecessors of twentieth-century art.

His last entry in his memoirs reads: "You see, I believe that we all are workers... Before all of us is the anvil and the hammer, and our duty is to forge [17]". Ever since he first took it up, Gauguin's "hammer", remained in his hand until his dying day.

64. *Still Life with Parrots*,
1902. Oil on canvas,
62 x 76 cm.
The Pushkin Museum
of Fine Arts, Moscow.